DUVALLS OSHA 1926

Instructors Manual
2014 Edition

Subpart A — General

OSHA Information. An edited report.

[Federal Register Volume 78, Number 78 (Tuesday, April 23, 2013)]
[Rules and Regulations]
[Pages 23837-23843]

From the Federal Register Online via Government Printing Office (www.gpo.gov)
[FR Doc No: 2013-09153]

Department of Labor Occupational Safety and Health Administration. 29 CFR Part 1926. [Docket No. OSHA-2007-0066] RIN No. 1218-AC61

Cranes and Derricks in Construction: Underground Construction and Demolition.

Agency: Occupational Safety and Health Administration (OSHA), Labor.

Action: Final rule.

SUMMARY: On August 17, 2012, OSHA issued a notice of proposed rulemaking, as well as a companion direct final rule, that proposed applying the requirements in OSHA's 2010 cranes and derricks construction standard to underground construction work and demolition work. The notice of proposed rulemaking also proposed to correct inadvertent errors in the underground construction and demolition standards. After receiving a comment recommending that OSHA clarify the proposed regulatory text of the demolition standard, OSHA clarified the text and is issuing this final rule to apply the cranes and derricks standard to underground construction work and demolition work.

Date: This final rule is effective May 23, 2013. Petitions for the final rule of this final review are due on June 24, 2013.

Publishers note:

This edition of 29 CFR OSHA Part §1926 Subpart A—General, is the annual review of DUVALLS OSHA 1926 Instructors Manual 2014 Edition. The updated OSHA information provided for Instructors for lecture purposes is current as of January, 2014. All Subparts of 1926 OSHA will be reviewed, corrected and updated for application as lecture and study information prior to publishing our multiple-choice test type questions with answers.

It is recognized that many test platforms and protocols requiring the use and application of OSHA textbooks, generally, are three to five years out of date in any given time frame. This situation is true in consideration of the normal government legislative process. In practice and application the publishing of Laws, Regulations and Rules requires extensive careful review before implementing enforcement.

It is the philosophy of Ficus Tree Publishing LLC. to provide the most current, up to date information to Instructors in the form of our Instructors Manuals for the purpose of providing this important and current supplemental study material to their students.

Intellectual Property Information:

United States Copyright Law and International Treaties prohibit unauthorized publication, distribution, reprinting, photocopying, of the whole, part, portion of this Work. Unauthorized publication, distribution, reprinting of any part, portion or whole of this document may result in severe criminal and civil penalties. All rights to this Work are reserved. Violations of this copyright are investigated by the United States Department of Justice and carry, upon conviction of fines up to $250,000 and five years confinement.

No part of this publication may be reproduced, distributed, posted, broadcast, digitalized, duplicated, photocopied, or electronically scanned by any means or methods, including, without limitation, optical, mechanical, electronic, photocopying, or recording by or in any information storage system, data information retrieval system or retrieval storage system without prior written permission of the author and publisher. Further, and in addition, purchasers of this document do not have the right or permission to republish, reprint, reproduce, photocopy, scan, digitalize, duplicate, post broadcast any or all of the information contained, thus presented herein, and within this document.

Although the Code of Regulations herein identified as 29 CFR OSHA PART 1926 Subparts **A**, B, C, D, E, F, G, H, I, J, K, L, M, N, O, P, Q, R, S, T, U, V, W, X, Y, Z and Subparts CC and DD are published by the United States of America, the creative work of researching, formatting, sequencing, developing, structuring the Work of the materials and information contained herein are subject to United States and International Treaties, copyright laws, codes and agreements.

While every effort has been made to ensure the information contained herein is accurate and complete at the time of publication the possibility of typographic errors, omissions, and/or oversights may exist. No patent liability is assumed with respect to the use of the information and material contained herein. This Work was created for use as a literary and educational study guide series in workbook format. This Work is a educational tool for the research, review, and study aid for and of the material and information presented herein. Thus and therefore, it is not the intent of the author or publisher that this work including the information and material contained herein shall be considered, applied, used as the definitive source for the information and material contained herein. Therefore, neither Ficus Tree Publishing, LLC or the author, nor any person or subsidiary thereof shall be liable for any damages resulting from the use, misuse, or reliance on this publication. In addition, this Work was not created or intended to be a stand-alone source document for the use or misuse by individuals, professional occupations, private or corporate entities or private provider educational entities.

Copyright information:

ISBN: 978-0-9895390-1-2

Publisher ID: 29CFROSHA1926MSGS-1-1926-2014-A

Author: DUVALL, JAMES W.

Title: DUVALLS OSHA 1926
              Instructors Manual 2014 Edition
              Subpart A—General
              A Master Study Guide Series

A Master Study Guide Series for 29 CFR OSHA PART 1926 Safety and Health Regulations For Construction Subpart A—General as published by the Office of the Federal Register National Archives and Records Administration.

This publication is intended solely as a Study Guide -Workbook Series, review and study aid to persons engaged in the study and application of the United States Department of Labor Safety and Health Regulations For Construction. This Work was not created for nor is it intended to be used as a stand-alone document for any business entity, profession, business enterprise, or similar private endeavor.

References: OSHA— Occupational Safety and Health Administration
and Source   Title: Subtitle B — Regulations Relating To Labor Part 1926 Safety and Health
Document   Regulations for Construction
                     Chapter XVII
                     U.S. Government Printing Office
                     U.S. Superintendent of Documents Washington, D.C. 204202-0001
                     http://bookstore.gpo.gov (888-512-1800)
                     LABOR 29 Part 1926
                     www.OSHA.gov

1926 Subpart A — General
Description

OSHA Part 1926 Subpart A—General. Part 1926 Subpart A—General is divided into five specific parts. § 1926.1 Purpose and scope. "(a) This part sets forth the safety and health standards promulgated by the Secretary of Labor under section 107 of the Contract Work Hours and Safety Standards Act." §1926.1(b). "Subpart B of this part contains statements of general policy and interpretations of section 107 of the Contract Work Hours and Safety Standards Act having general applicability."

§1926.1 Purpose and scope provides the Instructor with three (3) basic multiple-choice, test type questions with answers for lecture discussion or work assignment. The multiple-choice questions with answers follow the printed page sequence of the Department of Labor publication of 29 CFR Part 1926 Subpart A—General. **§1926.2** Variances from safety and health standards provides the Instructor with additional multiple-choice, test type questions with answers. §1926.2 has four (4) multiple-choice test type questions with answers relating to Variances. **§1926.3** Inspections—right of entry further expands the multiple-choice question set by five (5) additional exercises. The five questions continue to follow the basic test format relating to specific questions of the right of entry. **§1926.4** —Rules of practice for administrative adjudications for enforcement of safety and health standards; continues to increase by three (3) the multiple-choice, test type questions related to the basic, standard information contained in 1926 Subpart A—General. The above multiple-choice questions complete the basic outline of 1926 Subpart A—General. The following test type, multiple-choice questions with answers provide detailed study information for use by the Instructor to fit the lecture syllabus. The very detailed questions focus primarily on the OMB control numbers created and implemented for construction purposes under the Paperwork Reduction Act and the Implemented by reference part of §1926 Subpart A—General.

§1926 Test Sets A5, the **OMB control numbers** series of tests provides an extensive range of multiple-choice, test type questions with answers for the Instructor. Generally, there are 68 multiple-choice, test type questions available for the Instructor to select from this test series. The amount of questions may vary with the availability and requirements OSHA for this test series. The OMB numbers far exceed those required and listed in this OSHA publication.

§1926 Test Sets A6, Incorporation by reference. Due to the changing requirements set forth for 1926 OSHA an enlarged test series "Incorporation by reference" is added to this Master Study Guide. All questions for this test series have answers provided. Multiple-choice, test type questions will vary depending upon the official OSHA publication. Generally, 140 multiple-choice, test type questions with answers may be expected for §1926 Subpart A—General.

A note: The word "Act" — this is a statement that identifies this part as an "Act" of the Congress of the United States of America. This word "Act" thereby states that this is the law passed by both Houses of the Congress and Signed into law by the President of the United States. Who thus and therefore mandated the responsibility of creating the system of laws and regulations to the Secretary of Labor as published in the Congressional Record. In this 29 CFR OSHA Part 1926 are the Labor Laws - the regulations governing and regulating the safety and health of the United States Construction Industry.

Contents 1926 Subpart A—General

DU VALLS
OSHA 1926 Subpart A—General
Instructors Manual Master Study Guide Series
Test Set 1926 A1

29 CFR OSHA PART 1926 Subpart A—General

1. Subpart A §1926.1(a) Purpose and Scope.

1. (a) This part sets forth the safety and health standards promulgated by the Secretary of Labor under section ___ of the Contract Work Hours and Safety Standards Act.
    (a)   103
    (b)   105
    (c)   107
    (d)   109
    Answer: (c) 107 §1926.1(a) Subpart A Purpose and scope.

Subpart A §1926.1(a) Purpose and Scope.

2. (a) This part sets forth the safety and health standards promulgated by the Secretary of Labor under section ___ of the Contract Work Hours and Safety Standards Act. The standards are published in subpart ___ of this part and following subparts.
    (a)   103, A
    (b)   105, B
    (c)   107, C
    (d)   109, D
    Answer: (c) 107, C, §1926.1(a) Subpart A Purpose and scope.

Subpart A §1926.1(b) Purpose and Scope.

3. (b) Subpart ___ of this part contains statements of general policy and interpretations of section ___ of the Contract Work Hours and Safety Standards Act having general applicability.
    (a)   A, 105
    (b)   B, 107
    (c)   C, 110
    (d)   D, 1926
    Answer: (b) B, 107,§1926.1(b) Subpart A Purpose and scope.

2. Subpart A §1926.2(a) §1926.2 Variances from safety and health standards.

4. (a) Variances from standards which are, or may be, published in this part may be granted under ___ whereunder variances may be granted under section.
    (a)   the same circumstances
    (b)   similar circumstances
    (c)   comparable circumstances
    (d)   identical circumstances
    Answer: (a) the same circumstances, §1926.2(a) Variances from safety and health standards.

§1926.2(a) Subpart A §1926.2(a) §1926.2 Variances from safety and health standards.

5.   (a) Variances from standards which are, or may be, published in this part may be granted under the same circumstances whereunder variances may be granted under section 6(b)(A) or 6(d) of the ___ - ___ Occupational Safety and Health Act of 1970 (29 U.S.C 65). The procedures for the granting of variances and for related ___ under this part are those published in part ___ of this title.

    (a)   Hatfield-McCoy, events, 1902
    (b)   Davis-Bacon, Acts, 1903
    (c)   Taft-Hartley, acts, 1904
    (d)   Williams-Steiger, relief, 1905
    Answer: (d) Williams-Steiger, relief, 1905 §1926.2(a)

Subpart A §1926.2(b)

6.   (b) Any requests for variances under this section shall also be considered requests for variances under the Williams-Steiger Occupational Safety and Health Act with respect to ___ safety or health standards shall be considered to be also variances under the Construction Safety Act.

    (a)   job
    (b)   employee
    (c)   construction
    (d)   life
    Answer: (c) construction, §1926.2(b)

Subpart A §1926.2(b)

7.   (b) Any requests for variances under this section shall also be considered requests for variances under the ___-___ Occupational Safety and Health Act of 1970, and any requests for variances under ___-___ Occupational Safety and Health Act with respect to construction safety or health standards shall be considered to be also variances under the Construction Safety Act. Any variance from a construction safety or health standard which is contained in this part and which is incorporated by reference in Part 1910 of this title shall be deemed a variance from the standard under both the Construction Safety Act and the ___-___ Occupational Safety and Health Act of 1970.

    (a)   Williams-Steiger, Williams-Steiger, Williams-Steiger
    (b)   Davis-Bacon, Davis-Bacon, Davis-Bacon
    (c)   Taft-Hartley, Taft-Hartley, Taft-Hartley
    (d)   Hatfield-McCoy, Hatfield-McCoy, Hatfield-McCoy
    Answer: (a) Williams-Steiger §1926.2

3. Subpart A §1926.3 Inspections—right of entry.

8.   (a) It shall be a condition of each contract which is subject to section ___ of the Contract Work Hours and Safety Standards Act that the Secretary of labor or any authorized representative shall have a right of ____ to any site of contract performance for the following purposes:

(a)   107, entry
(b)   107, access
(c)   110, enter
(d)   110, inspection

Answer: (a) 107, entry §1926.3(a) Inspections — right of entry

Subpart A §1926.3(a)(1) Inspections—right to entry

9.   The paragraphs stated thus, (1) To inspect or investigate the manner of compliance with the safety and health standards contained in subpart ___ of this part and following subparts;

(a)   A
(b)   B
(c)   C
(d)   D

Answer: (c) C, 1926 Subpart A General §1926.3 (a)(1)

Subpart A §1926.3(a)(1)(2)

10.   The paragraphs stated thus, (1) To inspect or investigate the manner of compliance with the safety and health standards contained in subpart ___ of this part and following subparts; and (2) To carry out the duties of the Secretary under section ___ of the Act.

(a)   A, 107
(b)   B, 107(a)
(c)   C, 107(b)
(d)   D, 107(c)

Answer: (c) C, 107(b), 1926 Subpart A General §1926.3 (a)(1)(2)

Subpart A §1926.3(a)(1)(2)(b)

11.   The paragraphs stated thus, (1) To inspect or investigate the manner of compliance with the safety and health standards contained in subpart ___ of this part and following subparts; and (2) To carry out the duties of the Secretary under section ___ of the Act. (b) For the purpose of carrying out his investigative duties under the Act, the Secretary of Labor may, by agreement, use with or without ___ the services, personnel, and facilities of any State or Federal agency.

(a)   A, 107, payment
(b)   B, 107(a), compensation
(c)   C, 107(b), reimbursement
(d)   D, 107(c), financial recourse

Answer: (c) C, 107(b), reimbursement,1926 Subpart A General §1926.3 (a)(1)(2)(b)

Subpart A §1926.3(a)(1)(2)(b)

12.   The paragraphs stated thus, (1) To inspect or investigate the manner of compliance with the safety and health standards contained in subpart ___ of this part and following subparts; and (2) To carry out the duties of the Secretary under section ___ of the Act. (b) For the purpose of carrying out his investigative duties under the Act, the Secretary of Labor may, by agreement, use with or without ___ the services, personnel, and facilities of any State or Federal agency.

Any agreements with States under this ___ shall be similar to those provided for under the Walsh-Healey Public Contracts Act under 41 CFR part 50-205.

(a)   A, 107, payment, subpart
(b)   B, 107(a), compensation, part
(c)   C, 107(b), reimbursement, section
(d)   D, 107(c), financial recourse, subsection

Answer: (c) C, 107(b), reimbursement, section,1926 Subpart A General §1926.3 (a)(1)(2)(b)

4. Subpart A §1926.4 Rules of practice for administrative adjudications for law enforcement of safety and health standards.

Subpart A §1926.4(a)

13.　　(a) The rules of practice for administrative adjudications for the enforcement of safety and health standards contained in Subpart C of this part and the following subparts shall be the same as those published in Part ___ of this title with respect to safety and health violations of the Service Contract Act of ___ (69 Stat. 1035), except as provided in paragraph (b) of this section.

　　(a)　　4, 1950
　　(b)　　5, 1955
　　(c)　　6, 1965
　　(d)　　7, 1973

Answer: 6, 1965 §1926.4(a) Rules of practice for administrative adjudications for enforcement of safety and health standards.

Subpart A §1926.4(b)

14.　　(b) In the case of ___, the findings required by section 107(d) of the Act shall be made by the hearing examiner or the Assistant Secretary of Labor for Occupational safety and Health, as the case may be.

　　(a)　　disagreement
　　(b)　　debarred
　　(c)　　debarment
　　(d)　　disaster

Answer: (c) debarment, §1926.4(b) Rules of practice for administrative adjudications for enforcement of safety and health standards.

Subpart A §1926.4(b) Rules of practice

15.　　(b) In the case of ___, the findings required by section 107(d) of the Act shall be made by the hearing examiner or the Assistant Secretary of Labor for Occupational safety and Health, as the case may be. Whenever, as provided in section 107(2)(d), a contractor requests termination of debarment before the end of the ___-year period prescribed in that section, the request shall be filed in writing with the Assistant Secretary of Labor for Occupational Safety and Health who shall publish a notice in the FEDERAL REGISTER that the request has been received and ___ interested persons an opportunity to be heard upon the request, and thereafter the provisions of part ___ of this title shall apply with respect to prehearing conferences, hearings and related matters, and decisions and orders.

　　(a)　　disagreement, 1, contact, 4
　　(b)　　debarred, 2, notify, 5
　　(c)　　debarment, 3, afford, 6
　　(d)　　disaster, 4, allow, 7

Answer: (c) debarment, 3, afford, 6, §1926.4(b) Rules of practice for administrative adjudications for enforcement of safety and health standards.

A Ficus Tree Publishing LLC. Quick Notes Page

DU VALLS
OSHA 1926 Subpart A—General
Instructors Manual Master Study Guide Series
Test Set 1926.5 A1 OMB Control Numbers

5. OMB control numbers under the Paperwork Reduction Act.
   Subpart A §1926.5 OMB control numbers
1.   OMB defined means ___.
       (a)   Oversight Management Board
       (b)   Office of Management and Budget
       (c)   Office of Manpower and Labor
       (d)   Oversight Military Board
       Answer: (b) Office of Management and Budget

Subpart A §1926.5
2.   The following sections or paragraphs each contain a ___ of information requirements which has been approved by the Office of management and Budget under the control number listed.
       (a)   source
       (b)   valuable source
       (c)   file
       (d)   collection
       Answer: (d) collection

Subpart A §1926.5
3.   29 CFR citation 1926.33 OMB Control Number 1218-0065 is for a citation for violation of ___.
       (a)   Access to employee exposure and medical records
       (b)   Reorganization Plan No. 14
       (c)   Contract Work Hours
       (d)   Hazardous chemicals
       Answer: (a) Access to employee exposure and medical records. See §1926.33

Subpart A §1926.5
4.   29 CFR citation 1926.50 OMB Control Number 1218-0093 is for a citation for violation of ___.
       (a)   Medical services and first aid
       (b)   Masonry scaffold safety
       (c)   Steel erection safety
       (d)   Contract Work Hours
       Answer: (a) Medical services and first aid. See §1926.50

A Ficus Tree Publishing LLC., Educational - Technical Publication

Subpart A §1926.5 OMB control numbers
5.   29 CFR citation 1926.52 OMB Control Number 1218-0048 is for a citation for violation of ___.
    (a)   Medical services and first aid
    (b)   Masonry scaffold safety
    (c)   Occupational noise exposure
    (d)   Contract Work Hours
Answer: (c) Occupational noise exposure. See §1926.52

Subpart A §1926.5
6.   29 CFR citation 1926.53 OMB Control Number 1218-0103 is for a citation for violation of ___.
    (a)   Medical services and first aid
    (b)   Masonry scaffold safety
    (c)   Steel erection safety
    (d)   Ionizing radiation
Answer: (d) Ionizing radiation. See §1926.53

Subpart A §1926.5
7.   29 CFR citation 1926.59 OMB Control Number 1218-0072 is for a citation for violation of ___.
    (a)   Medical services and first aid
    (b)   Masonry scaffold safety
    (c)   Hazard communication
    (d)   Ionizing radiation
Answer: (c) Hazard communication. See §1926.59

Subpart A §1926.5
8.   29 CFR citation 1926.60 OMB Control Number 1218-0172 is for a citation for violation of ___.
    (a)   Methylenedianiline
    (b)   Chlorine Dioxide
    (c)   Bromine
    (d)   Ammonia
Answer: (a) Methylenedianiline. See §1926.60

Subpart A §1926.5
9.   29 CFR citation 1926.62 OMB Control Number 1218-0189 is for a citation for violation of ___.
    (a)   Lead
    (b)   Chlorine Dioxide
    (c)   Bromine
    (d)   Ammonia
Answer: (a) Lead. See §1926.62

Subpart A §1926.5 OMB control numbers
10.   29 CFR citation 1926.64 OMB Control Number 1218-0200 is for a citation for violation
of ___.
(a)   Lead
(b)   Process safety management of highly hazardous chemicals
(c)   Bromine
(d)   Ammonia
Answer: (b) Process safety management of highly hazardous chemicals. See §1926.64

Subpart A §1926.5
11.   29 CFR citation 1926.65 OMB Control Number 1218-0202 is for a citation for violation
of ___.
(a)   Lead
(b)   Process safety management of highly hazardous chemicals
(c)   Hazardous waste operation and emergency response
(d)   Ammonia
Answer: (c) Hazardous waste operation and emergency response. See §1926.65

Subpart A §1926.5
12.   29 CFR citation 1926.103 OMB Control Number 1218-0099 is for a citation for violation
of ___.
(a)   Lead
(b)   Process safety management of highly hazardous chemicals
(c)   Hazardous waste operation and emergency response
(d)   Respiratory protection
Answer: (d) Respiratory protection. See §1926.103

Subpart A §1926.5
13.   29 CFR citation 1926.200 OMB Control Number 1218-0132 is for a citation for violation
of ___.
(a)   Accident prevention signs and tags
(b)   Process safety management of highly hazardous chemicals
(c)   Hazardous waste operation and emergency response
(d)   Respiratory protection
Answer: (a) Accident prevention signs and tags. See §1926.200

Subpart A §1926.5
14.   29 CFR citation 1926.250 OMB Control Number 1218-0093 is for a citation for violation
of ___.
(a)   Accident prevention signs and tags
(b)   General requirements for storage
(c)   Hazardous waste operation and emergency response
(d)   Respiratory protection
Answer: (b) General requirements for storage. See §1926.250

Subpart A §1926.5 OMB control numbers
15.   29 CFR citation 1926.251 OMB Control Number 1218-0233 is for a citation for violation of ___.
   (a)   Accident prevention signs and tags
   (b)   General requirements for storage
   (c)   Rigging equipment for material handling
   (d)   Respiratory protection
   Answer: (c) Rigging equipment for material handling. See §1926.251

Subpart A §1926.5
16.   29 CFR citation 1926.403 OMB Control Number 1218-0130 is for a citation for violation of ___.
   (a)   Accident prevention signs and tags
   (b)   General requirements for storage
   (c)   Rigging equipment for material handling
   (d)   General requirements
   Answer: (d) General requirements. See §1926.403

Subpart A §1926.5
17.   29 CFR citation 1926.404 OMB Control Number 1218-0130 is for a citation for violation of ___.
   (a)   Wiring design and protection
   (b)   General requirements for storage
   (c)   Rigging equipment for material handling
   (d)   General requirements
   Answer: (a) Wiring design and protection. See §1926.404

Subpart A §1926.5
18.   29 CFR citation 1926.405 OMB Control Number 1218-0130 is for a citation for violation of ___.
   (a)   Wiring design and protection
   (b)   Wiring methods, components, and equipment for general use
   (c)   Rigging equipment for material handling
   (d)   General requirements
   Answer: (b) Wiring methods, components, and equipment for general use. See §1926.405

Subpart A §1926.5
19.   29 CFR citation 1926.407 OMB Control Number 1218-0130 is for a citation for violation of ___.
   (a)   Wiring design and protection
   (b)   Wiring methods, components, and equipment for general use
   (c)   Hazardous (classified) locations
   (d)   General requirements
   Answer: (c) Hazardous (classified) locations. See §1926.407

Subpart A §1926.5 OMB control numbers
20.   29 CFR citation 1926.408 OMB Control Number 1218-0130 is for a citation for violation of ___.
(a)   Wiring design and protection
(b)   Wiring methods, components, and equipment for general use
(c)   Hazardous (classified) locations
(d)   Special systems
Answer: (d) Special systems. See §1926.408

Subpart A §1926.5
21.   29 CFR citation 1926.453(a)(2) OMB Control Number 1218-0216 is for a citation for violation of ___.
(a)   Extensible and articulating boom platforms
(b)   Wiring methods, components, and equipment for general use
(c)   Hazardous (classified) locations
(d)   Special systems
Answer: (a) Extensible and articulating boom platforms. See §1926.453(a)(2)

Subpart A §1926.5
22.   29 CFR citation 1926.502 OMB Control Number 1218-0197 is for a citation for violation of ___.
(a)   Aerial lifts
(b)   Fall protection systems criteria and practices
(c)   Hazardous (classified) locations
(d)   Special systems
Answer: (b) Fall protection systems and practices. See §1926.502

Subpart A §1926.5
23.   29 CFR citation 1926.503 OMB Control Number 1218-0197 is for a citation for violation of ___.
(a)   Aerial lifts
(b)   Fall protection systems criteria and practices
(c)   Training requirements
(d)   Special systems
Answer: (c) Training requirements. See §1926.503

Subpart A §1926.5
24.   29 CFR citation 1926.550(a)(1) OMB Control Number 1218-0115 is for a citation for violation of ___.
(a)   Aerial lifts
(b)   Fall protection systems criteria and practices
(c)   Training requirements
(d)   General requirements
Answer: (d) General requirements. See §1926.550(a)(1)

Subpart A §1926.5 OMB control numbers
25. 29 CFR citation 1926.550(a)(2) OMB Control Number 1218-0115 is for a citation for violation of ___.
   (a) Rated load capacities
   (b) Fall protection systems criteria and practices
   (c) Training requirements
   (d) General requirements
   Answer: (a) Rated load capacities. See §1926.550(a)(2)

Subpart A §1926.5
26. 29 CFR citation 1926.550(a)(4) OMB Control Number 1218-0115 is for a citation for violation of ___.
   (a) Rated load capacities
   (b) Hand signals to crane and derrick operators
   (c) Training requirements
   (d) General requirements
   Answer: (b) Hand signals to crane and derrick operators. See §1926.550(a)(4)

Subpart A §1926.5
27. 29 CFR citation 1926.550(a)(6) OMB Control Number 1218-0113 is for a citation for violation of ___.
   (a) Rated load capacities
   (b) Hand signals to crane and derrick operators
   (c) A thorough, annual inspection of the hoisting machinery shall be made by a competent person, or
   (d) General requirements
   Answer: (c) A thorough, annual inspection of the hoisting machinery shall be made by a competent person, or. See §1926.550(a)(6)

Subpart A §1926.5
28. 29 CFR citation 1926.550(a)(11) OMB Control Number 1218-0054 is for a citation for violation of ___.
   (a) Rated load capacities
   (b) Hand signals to crane and derrick operators
   (c) A thorough, annual inspection of the hoisting machinery shall be made by a competent person, or
   (d) Whenever internal combustion engine powered equipment exhausts in enclosed spaces, tests shall be made and recorded/
   Answer: (d) Whenever internal combustion engine powered equipment exhausts in enclosed spaces, tests shall be made and recorded/ See §1926.550(a)(11)

DU VALLS
OSHA 1925 Subpart A—General
Instructors Manual Master Study Guide Series
Test Set 1926.5 A2 OMB control numbers

Subpart A §1926.5 OMB control numbers

1.	29 CFR citation 1926.550(a)(16) OMB Control Number 1218-0115 is for a citation for violation of ___.
	(a)	No modifications or additions which affect the capacity or safe operation shall be made to the equipment without the manufacture's written approval.
	(b)	Hand signals to crane and derrick operators
	(c)	A thorough, annual inspection of the hoisting machinery shall be made by a competent person, or
	(d)	Whenever internal combustion engine powered equipment exhausts in enclosed spaces, tests shall be made and recorded/

	Answer: (a) No modifications or additions which affect the capacity or safe operation shall be made to the equipment without the manufacture's written approval. See §1926.550(a)(16)

Subpart A §1926.5

2.	29 CFR citation 1926.550(b)(2) OMB Control Number 1218-0232 is for a citation for violation of ___.
	(a)	No modifications or additions which affect the capacity or safe operation shall be made to the equipment without the manufacture's written approval.
	(b)	All crawler, truck, or locomotive cranes in use shall meet the applicable requirements for design, inspection, construction, testing, maintenance and operation as prescribed in ANSI B30.5-1968
	(c)	A thorough, annual inspection of the hoisting machinery shall be made by a competent person, or
	(d)	Whenever internal combustion engine powered equipment exhausts in enclosed spaces, tests shall be made and recorded/

	Answer: (b) All crawler, truck, or locomotive cranes in use shall meet the applicable requirements for design, inspection, construction, testing, maintenance and operation as prescribed in ANSI B30.5-1968. See §1926.550(b)(2)

Subpart A §1926.5. OMB numbers

3.   29 CFR citation 1926.550(g) OMB Control Number 1218-0151 is for a citation for violation of ___.

  (a)   No modifications or additions which affect the capacity or safe operation shall be made to the equipment without the manufacture's written approval.

  (b)   All crawler, truck, or locomotive cranes in use shall meet the applicable requirements for design, inspection, construction, testing, maintenance and operation as prescribed in ANSI B30.5-1968

  (c)   Crane or derrick suspended platform

  (d)   Whenever internal combustion engine powered equipment exhausts in enclosed spaces, tests shall be made and recorded/

Answer: (c) Crane or derrick suspended platform. See §1926.550(g)

Subpart A §1926.5

4.   29 CFR citation 1926.552 OMB Control Number 1218-0151 is for a citation for violation of ___.

  (a)   No modifications or additions which affect the capacity or safe operation shall be made to the equipment without the manufacture's written approval.

  (b)   All crawler, truck, or locomotive cranes in use shall meet the applicable requirements for design, inspection, construction, testing, maintenance and operation as prescribed in ANSI B30.5-1968

  (c)   Crane or derrick suspended platform

  (d)   Material hoists, personnel hoists, and elevators

Answer: (d) Material hoists, personnel hoists, and elevators. See §1926.552

Subpart A §1926.5

5.   29 CFR citation 1926.652 OMB Control Number 1218-0137 is for a citation for violation of ___.

  (a)   Requirements for protective systems

  (b)   All crawler, truck, or locomotive cranes in use shall meet the applicable requirements for design, inspection, construction, testing, maintenance and operation as prescribed in ANSI B30.5-1968

  (c)   Crane or derrick suspended platform

  (d)   Material hoists, personnel hoists, and elevators

Answer: (a) Requirements for protective systems. See §1926.652

Subpart A §1926.5

6.   29 CFR citation 1926.703 OMB Control Number 1218-0095 is for a citation for violation of ___.

  (a)   Requirements for protective systems

  (b)   Requirements for cast-in-place concrete

  (c)   Crane or derrick suspended platform

  (d)   Material hoists, personnel hoists, and elevators

Answer: (b) Requirements for cast-in-place concrete. See §1926.703

Subpart A §1926.5 OMB control numbers

7. 29 CFR citation 1926.800 OMB Control Number 1218-0067 is for a citation for violation of ___.
   (a) Requirements for protective systems
   (b) Requirements for cast-in-place concrete
   (c) Underground construction
   (d) Material hoists, personnel hoists, and elevators
   Answer: (c) Underground construction. See §1926.800

Subpart A §1926.5

8. 29 CFR citation 1926.803 OMB Control Number 1218-0067 is for a citation for violation of ___.
   (a) Requirements for protective systems
   (b) Requirements for cast-in-place concrete
   (c) Underground construction
   (d) Material hoists, personnel hoists, and elevators
   Answer: (c) Underground construction. See §1926.803

Subpart A §1926.5

9. 29 CFR citation 1926.900 OMB Control Number 1218-0217 is for a citation for violation of ___.
   (a) Requirements for protective systems
   (b) Requirements for cast-in-place concrete
   (c) Underground construction
   (d) General provisions
   Answer: (d) General provisions. See §1926.900

Subpart A §1926.5

10. 29 CFR citation 1926.903 OMB Control Number 1218-0227 is for a citation for violation of ___.
    (a) Underground transportation of explosives
    (b) Requirements for cast-in-place concrete
    (c) Underground construction
    (d) General provisions
    Answer: (a) Underground transportation of explosives. See §1926.903

Subpart A §1926.5

11. 29 CFR citation 1926.1080 OMB Control Number 1218-0069 is for a citation for violation of ___.
    (a) Underground transportation of explosives
    (b) Safe practices manual
    (c) Underground construction
    (d) General provisions
    Answer: (b) Safe practices manual. See §1926.1080

Subpart A §1926.5 OMB control numbers
12.   29 CFR citation 1926.1081 OMB Control Number 1218-0069 is for a citation for violation of ___.
    (a)   Underground transportation of explosives
    (b)   Safe practices manual
    (c)   Pre-dive procedures
    (d)   General provisions
Answer: (c) Pre-dive procedures. See §1926.1081

Subpart A §1926.5
13.   29 CFR citation 1926.1083 OMB Control Number 1218-0069 is for a citation for violation of ___.
    (a)   Underground transportation of explosives
    (b)   Safe practices manual
    (c)   Pre-dive procedures
    (d)   Post-dive procedures
Answer: (d) Post-dive procedures. See §1926.1083

Subpart A §1926.5
14.   29 CFR citation 1926.1090 OMB Control Number 1218-0069 is for a citation for violation of ___.
    (a)   Equipment
    (b)   Safe practices manual
    (c)   Pre-dive procedures
    (d)   Post-dive procedures
Answer: (a) Equipment. See §1926.1090

Subpart A §1926.5
15.   29 CFR citation 1926.1091 OMB Control Number 1218-0069 is for a citation for violation of ___.
    (a)   Recordkeeping requirements
    (b)   Safe practices manual
    (c)   Pre-dive procedures
    (d)   Post-dive procedures
Answer: (a) Recordkeeping requirements. See §1926.1091

Subpart A §1926.5
16.   29 CFR citation 1926.1101 OMB Control Number 1218-0134 is for a citation for violation of ___.
    (a)   Equipment
    (b)   Safe practices manual
    (c)   Asbestos
    (d)   Post-dive procedures
Answer: (c) Asbestos. See §1926.1101

Subpart A §1926.5 OMB control numbers
17.   29 CFR citation 1926.1101 OMB Control Number 1218-0134 is for a citation for
       violation of ___.
       (a)   Equipment
       (b)   Safe practices manual
       (c)   Asbestos
       (d)   Post-dive procedures
       Answer: (c) Asbestos. See §1926.1101

Subpart A §1926.5 OMB control numbers - Toxic and Hazardous Substances
18.   A 29 CFR citation issued for a violation of 1926.1103 OMB Number 1218-0085 is a
       violation of the safety provisions governing Subpart Z. Specifically ___.
       (a)   Asbestos
       (b)   Ethylene
       (c)   alpha-Naphthylamine
       (d)   13 carcinogens(4 Nitrobiphenyl, etc.)
       Answer: (d) 13 carcinogens(4 Nitrobiphenyl, etc.) §1926.1103 Z — Toxic and Hazardous
       Substances

Subpart A §1926.5
19.   A 29 CFR citation issued for a violation of 1926.1104 OMB Number 1218-0084 is a
       violation of the safety provisions governing Subpart Z. Specifically ___.
       (a)   Asbestos
       (b)   Ethylene
       (c)   alpha-Naphthylamine
       (d)   13 carcinogens(4 Nitrobiphenyl, etc.)
       Answer: (c) alpha-Naphthylamine §1926.1104 Z — Toxic and Hazardous Substances

Subpart A §1926.5
20.   A 29 CFR citation issued for a violation of 1926.1106 OMB Number 1218-0086 is a
       violation of the safety provisions governing Subpart Z. Specifically ___.
       (a)   Methyl chloromethyl ether
       (b)   Ethylene
       (c)   alpha-Naphthylamine
       (d)   13 carcinogens(4 Nitrobiphenyl, etc.)
       Answer: (a) Methyl chloromethyl ether §1926.1106 Z — Toxic and Hazardous
       Substances

Subpart A §1926.5
21.   A 29 CFR citation issued for a violation of 1926.1107 OMB Number 1218-0083 is a
       violation of the safety provisions governing Subpart Z. Specifically ___.
       (a)   Methyl chloromethyl ether
       (b)   3,3'-Dichlorobenzidiene
       (c)   alpha-Naphthylamine
       (d)   13 carcinogens(4 Nitrobiphenyl, etc.)
       Answer: (b) 3,3'-Dichlorobenzidiene §1926.1107 Z — Toxic and Hazardous Substances

Subpart A §1926.5 OMB control numbers - Toxic and Hazardous Substances

22.   29 CFR citation 1926.1108 OMB Control Number 1218-0087 is for a citation for violation of ___.
   (a)   Equipment
   (b)   Safe practices manual
   (c)   Asbestos
   (d)   bis-Chloromethyl ether
   Answer: (d) bis-Chloromethyl ether. See §1926.1108 Z — Toxic and Hazardous Substances

Subpart A §1926.5

23.   29 CFR citation 1926.1109 OMB Control Number 1218-0089 is for a citation for violation of ___.
   (a)   beta-Naphthylamine
   (b)   Safe practices manual
   (c)   Asbestos
   (d)   bis-Chloromethyl ether
   Answer: (a) beta-Naphthylamine. See §1926.1109 Z — Toxic and Hazardous Substances

Subpart A §1926.5

24.   A 29 CFR citation issued for a violation of 1926.1110 OMB Number 1218-0082 is a violation of the safety provisions governing Subpart Z. Specifically ___.
   (a)   Methyl chloromethyl ether
   (b)   3,3'-Dichlorobenzidiene
   (c)   Benzidine
   (d)   13 carcinogens(4 Nitrobiphenyl, etc.)
   Answer: (c) Benzidine §1926.1110 Z — Toxic and Hazardous Substances

Subpart A §1926.5

25.   A 29 CFR citation issued for a violation of 1926.1111 OMB Number 1218-0090 is a violation of the safety provisions governing Subpart Z. Specifically ___.
   (a)   Methyl chloromethyl ether
   (b)   3,3'-Dichlorobenzidiene
   (c)   Benzidine
   (d)   4-Aminodiphenyl
   Answer: (d) 4-Aminodiphenyl §1926.1111 Z — Toxic and Hazardous Substances

Subpart A §1926.5

26.   A 29 CFR citation issued for a violation of 1926.1112 OMB Number 1218-0080 is a violation of the safety provisions governing Subpart Z. Specifically ___.
   (a)   Ethyleneimine
   (b)   3,3'-Dichlorobenzidiene
   (c)   Benzidine
   (d)   4-Aminodiphenyl
   Answer: (a) Ethyleneimine §1926.1112 Z — Toxic and Hazardous Substances

Subpart A §1926.5 OMB control numbers - Toxic and Hazardous Substances
27.   A 29 CFR citation issued for a violation of 1926.1113 OMB Number 1218-0079 is a violation of the safety provisions governing Subpart Z. Specifically ___.
    (a)   Ethyleneimine
    (b)   beta-Propiolactone
    (c)   Benzidine
    (d)   4-Aminodiphenyl
    Answer: (b) beta-Propiolactone. §1926.1113 Z — Toxic and Hazardous Substances

Subpart A §1926.5
28.   A 29 CFR citation issued for a violation of 1926.1114 OMB Number 1218-0088 is a violation of the safety provisions governing Subpart Z. Specifically ___.
    (a)   Ethyleneimine
    (b)   beta-Propiolactone
    (c)   2-Acetyaminofluorene
    (d)   4-Aminodiphenyl
    Answer: (c) 2-Acetyaminofluorene beta-Propiolactone. §1926.1114 Z — Toxic and Hazardous Substances

Subpart A §1926.5
29.   A 29 CFR citation issued for a violation of 1926.1115 OMB Number 1218-0044 is a violation of the safety provisions governing Subpart Z. Specifically ___.
    (a)   Ethyleneimine
    (b)   beta-Propiolactone
    (c)   2-Acetyaminofluorene
    (d)   4-Dimethylaminoazobenzene
    Answer: (d) 4-Dimethylaminoazobenzene. §1926.1115 Z — Toxic and Hazardous Substances

Subpart A §1926.5
30.   A 29 CFR citation issued for a violation of 1926.1116 OMB Number 1218-0081 is a violation of the safety provisions governing Subpart Z. Specifically ___.
    (a)   N-Nitrosodimethylamine
    (b)   beta-Propiolactone
    (c)   2-Acetyaminofluorene
    (d)   4-Dimethylaminoazobenzene
    Answer: (a) N-Nitrosodimethylamine. §1926.1116 Z — Toxic and Hazardous Substances

Subpart A §1926.5
31.   A 29 CFR citation issued for a violation of 1926.1117 OMB Number 1218-0010 is a violation of the safety provisions governing Subpart Z. Specifically ___.
    (a)   Ethyleneimine
    (b)   beta-Propiolactone
    (c)   2-Acetyaminofluorene
    (d)   Vinyl chloride
    Answer: (d) Vinyl chloride. §1926.1117 Z — Toxic and Hazardous Substances

Subpart A §1926.5 OMB control numbers

32.   A 29 CFR citation issued for a violation of 1926.1118 OMB Number 1218-0104 is a violation of the safety provisions governing Subpart Z. Specifically ___.
  (a)   Inorganic arsenic
  (b)   beta-Propiolactone
  (c)   2-Acetyaminofluorene
  (d)   N-Nitrosodimethylamine
  Answer: (a) Inorganic arsenic. §1926.1118 Z — Toxic and Hazardous Substances

Subpart A §1926.5

33.   A 29 CFR citation issued for a violation of 1926.1126 OMB Number 1218-0252 is a violation of the safety provisions governing Subpart Z. Specifically ___.
  (a)   Inorganic arsenic
  (b)   Chromium (VI)
  (c)   2-Acetyaminofluorene
  (d)   N-Nitrosodimethylamine
  Answer: (b) Chromium (VI) arsenic. §1926.1126 Z — Toxic and Hazardous Substances

Subpart A §1926.5

34.   A 29 CFR citation issued for a violation of 1926.1127 OMB Number 1218-0186 is a violation of the safety provisions governing Subpart Z. Specifically ___.
  (a)   Inorganic arsenic
  (b)   beta-Propiolactone
  (c)   Cadmium
  (d)   N-Nitrosodimethylamine
  Answer: (c) Cadmium. §1926.1127 Z — Toxic and Hazardous Substances

Subpart A §1926.5

35.   A 29 CFR citation issued for a violation of 1926.1128 OMB Number 1218-0129 is a violation of the safety provisions governing Subpart Z. Specifically ___.
  (a)   Inorganic arsenic
  (b)   beta-Propiolactone
  (c)   Cadmium
  (d)   Benzene
  Answer: (d) Benzene. §1926.1128 Z — Toxic and Hazardous Substances

Subpart A §1926.5

36.   A 29 CFR citation issued for a violation of 1926.1129 OMB Number 1218-0128 is a violation of the safety provisions governing Subpart Z. Specifically ___.
  (a)   Inorganic arsenic
  (b)   Coke oven emissions
  (c)   Cadmium
  (d)   Benzene
  Answer: (b) Coke oven emissions. §1926.1129 Z — Toxic and Hazardous Substances

Subpart A §1926.5 OMB control numbers - Toxic and Hazardous Substances
37.   A 29 CFR citation issued for a violation of 1926.1144 OMB Number 1218-0101 is a violation of the safety provisions governing Subpart Z. Specifically ___.
(a)   1,2-dibromo-3-chloropropane
(b)   Coke oven emissions
(c)   Cadmium
(d)   Benzene
Answer: (a) 1,2-dibromo-3-chloropropane. §1926.1144 Z — Toxic and Hazardous Substances

Subpart A §1926.5
38.   A 29 CFR citation issued for a violation of 1926.1145 OMB Number 1218-0126 is a violation of the safety provisions governing Subpart Z. Specifically ___.
(a)   1,2-dibromo-3-chloropropane
(b)   Acrylonitrile
(c)   Cadmium
(d)   Benzene
Answer: (b) Acrylonitrile. §1926.1145 Z — Toxic and Hazardous Substances

Subpart A §1926.5
39.   A 29 CFR citation issued for a violation of 1926.1147 OMB Number 1218-0108 is a violation of the safety provisions governing Subpart Z. Specifically ___.
(a)   1,2-dibromo-3-chloropropane
(b)   Acrylonitrile
(c)   Ethylene oxide
(d)   Benzene
Answer: (c) Ethylene oxide. §1926.1147 Z — Toxic and Hazardous Substances

Subpart A §1926.5
40.   A 29 CFR citation issued for a violation of 1926.1148 OMB Number 1218-0145 is a violation of the safety provisions governing Subpart Z. Specifically ___.
(a)   1,2-dibromo-3-chloropropane
(b)   Acrylonitrile
(c)   Ethylene oxide
(d)   Methylene chloride
Answer: (d) Methylene chloride. §1926.1148 Z — Toxic and Hazardous Substances

Authority: 40 U.S.C. 333; 29 U.S.C. 653, 655, 657; Secretary of Labor's Order No. 12-71 (36 FR 8754), 8-76 (41 FR 25059), 9-83 (48 FR 35736), 6-96 (62- FR 111) 5-2007 (72 FR 31160), 4-2010 (77 FR 3912), as applicable; and 29 CFR part 1911.
[61 FR 5509, Feb.13, 1996, as amended at 63 FR 3814, Jan. 27, 1998; 63 FR 13340, Mar. 19, 1998; 63 FR 17094, Apr. 8, 1998; 64 FR 18810, Apr. 16, 1999; 71 FR 38096, July 5, 2006; 75 FR 12686, March 17, 2010; 75 FR 48130, Aug. 9, 2010; 75 FR 68430, Nov. 8, 2010; 77 FR 37600, June 22, 2012; 78 FR 35566, June 13, 2013; **78 FR 66641, November 6, 2013**]

A Ficus Tree Publishing LLC. Quick Notes Page

DU VALLS
OSHA 1926 Subpart A—General
Instructors MANUAL Master Study Guide Series
29 CFR LABOR OSHA Part 1926 Subpart A — General
Test Set 1926.6 A1—Incorporation by reference

Subpart A §1926.6(a) Incorporation by reference

1. The standards of agencies of the U.S. Government, and organizations which are not agencies of the U.S. Government which are incorporated by reference in this part, have the ___ and effect as other standards in this part.
    (a)   authority
    (b)   force
    (c)   legal standing
    (d)   same force
    Answer: (d) same force. See §1926.6(a)

Subpart A §1926.6(a)

2. The standards of agencies of the U.S. Government, and organizations which are not agencies of the U.S. Government which are incorporated by reference in this part, have the ___ and effect as other standards in this part. Only the ___ provisions (i.e., provisions containing the word "shall" or other ___ language) of standards incorporated by reference are adopted as standards under the Occupational Safety and Health Act.
    (a)   authority, same force, legal standing
    (b)   force, force, legal standing
    (c)   legal standing, force, same force
    (d)   same force, mandatory, mandatory
    Answer: (d) same force, mandatory, mandatory. See §1926.6(a)

Subpart A §1926.6(a)

3. The standards of agencies of the U.S. Government, and organizations which are not agencies of the U.S. Government which are incorporated by reference in this part, have the ___ and effect as other standards in this part. Only the ___ provisions (i.e., provisions containing the word "shall" or other ___ language) of standards incorporated by reference are adopted as standards under the Occupational Safety and Health Act. The ___ where these standards may be examined are as follows:
    (a)   authority, same force, legal standing, office
    (b)   force, force, legal standing, office
    (c)   legal standing, force, same force, site
    (d)   same force, mandatory, mandatory, locations
    Answer: (d) same force, mandatory, mandatory, locations. See §1926.6(a)

Subpart A §1926.6(a)(1) Incorporation by reference

4.   The standards of agencies of the U.S. Government, and organizations which are not agencies of the U.S. Government which are incorporated by reference in this part, have the same force and effect as other standards in this part. Only the mandatory provisions (i.e., provisions containing the word "shall" or other mandatory language) of standards incorporated by reference are adopted as standards under the Occupational Safety and Health Act. The locations where these standards may be examined are as follows: Offices of the Occupational Safety and Health Administration, U.S. Department of labor, ___ Perkins Building, Washington, DC 20210.

(a)   Barbara
(b)   Frances
(c)   Robert
(d)   Susan

Answer: (b) Frances. See §1926.6(a)(1)

Subpart A §1926.6(a)(2)

5.   The standards of agencies of the U.S. Government, and organizations which are not agencies of the U.S. Government which are incorporated by reference in this part, have the same force and effect as other standards in this part. Only the mandatory provisions (i.e., provisions containing the word "shall" or other mandatory language) of standards incorporated by reference are adopted as standards under the Occupational Safety and Health Act. The locations where these standards may be examined are as follows: The Regional and ___ Offices of the Occupational Safety and Health Administration, which are listed in the U.S. Government Manual.

(a)   local
(b)   official
(c)   Regional
(d)   Registered

Answer: (c) Regional. See §1926.6(a)(2)

Subpart A §1926.6(b)

6.   The materials listed in paragraphs (___) through (___) of this section are incorporated by reference in the corresponding sections noted as they exist on the date of the approval, and a notice of any change in these materials will be published in the **Federal Register**.

(a)   a, d
(b)   a, g
(c)   g, ff
(d)   ff, tt

Answer: (c) g, ff. See §1926.6(b)

Subpart A §1926.6(b) Incorporation by reference
7.	The materials listed in paragraphs (___) through (___) of this section are incorporated by reference in the corresponding sections noted as they exist on the date of the approval, and a notice of any change in these materials will be published in the **Federal Register**. These incorporations by reference were approved by the Director of the ___ in accordance with 5 U.S.C. 552(a) and 1 CFR part 51.
	(a)	a, d, **Federal Register**
	(b)	a, g, Labor
	(c)	g, ff, Federal Register
	(d)	ff, tt, **Labor**
	Answer: (c) g, ff, Federal Register. See §1926.6(b)

Subpart A §1926.6(c)
8.	Copies of standards listed in this section and issued by private standards organizations are available for purchase from the ___ at the addresses or through the other information listed below for these private standards organizations.
	(a)	issuing office
	(b)	responsible individual
	(c)	bookstore
	(d)	issuing organizations
	Answer: (d) issuing organizations. See §1926.6(c)

Subpart A §1926.6(c)
9.	Copies of standards listed in this section and issued by private standards organizations are available for purchase from the ___ at the addresses or through the other information listed below for these private standards organizations. In addition, these standards are available for ___ at the National Archives and Records Administration (NARA).
	(a)	issuing office, ordering
	(b)	responsible individual, purchase
	(c)	bookstore, purchase
	(d)	issuing organizations, inspection
	Answer: (d) issuing organizations, inspection. See §1926.6(c)

Subpart A §1926.6(c)
10.	Copies of standards listed in this section and issued by private standards organizations are available for purchase from the ___ at the addresses or through the other information listed below for these private standards organizations. In addition, these standards are available for ___ at the National Archives and Records Administration (NARA).For information on the availability of these standards at ___ , telephone:
	(a)	issuing office, ordering, FUTA
	(b)	responsible individual, purchase, NCAA
	(c)	bookstore, purchase, OSHA
	(d)	issuing organizations, inspection, NARA
	Answer: (d) issuing organizations, inspection. See §1926.6(c)

Subpart A §1926.6(c) Incorporation by reference

11.   Copies of standards listed in this section and issued by private standards organizations are available for purchase from the issuing organizations at the addresses or through the other information listed below for these private standards organizations. In addition, these standards are available for inspection at the National Archives and Records Administration (NARA).For information on the availability of these standards at NARA , telephone: 202-741-6030, or go to

http://www.archives.gov/federal_register/code_of_federal_regulations_locations.html. Also, the standards are available for ___ at any Regional Office of the Occupational safety and Health Administration (OSHA), or at the Docket Office, U.S. Department of Labor, 200 Constitution Avenue, NW

(a)   review
(b)   examination
(c)   inspection
(d)   reading
Answer: (c) inspection. See §1926.6(c)

Subpart A §1926.6(c)

12.   Copies of standards listed in this section and issued by private standards organizations are available for purchase from the issuing organizations at the addresses or through the other information listed below for these private standards organizations. In addition, these standards are available for inspection at the National Archives and Records Administration (NARA).For information on the availability of these standards at NARA , telephone: 202-741-6030, or go to

http://www.archives.gov/federal_register/code_of_federal_regulations_locations.html. Also, the standards are available for ___ at any Regional Office of the Occupational safety and Health Administration (OSHA), or at the Docket Office, U.S. Department of Labor, 200 Constitution Avenue, NW., Room ___, Washington, DC 20210; telephone (TTY number: 877-889-5627).

(a)   review, 1652
(b)   examination, 1655
(c)   inspection, 2625
(d)   reading, 3353
Answer: (c) inspection, 2625. See §1926.6(c)

Subpart A §1926.6(d)

13.   1926.6(d), 1926.6(e), 1926.6(f) are listed as ___.
(a)   Reserved
(b)   Unavailable
(c)   Removed
(d)   [Reserved]
Answer: (d) [Reserved] See §1926.6(d),(e), (f).

A. Alphabetical listing—Incorporation by reference
Subpart A §1926.6(g) Incorporation by reference
14.   The following material is available for ___ from the American Conference of
        Governmental Industrial Hygienists (**ACGIH**), 1330 Kemper meadow Drive, Cincinnati,
        OH 45240; telephone 513-742-3355; email: *mail@acgih.org*
        (a)   reordering
        (b)   purchase
        (c)   review
        (d)   examination
        Answer: (b) purchase. See §1926.6(g)

Subpart A §1926.6(g)(1)
15.   Threshold Limit Values of Airborne Contaminants for 1970, 1970,IBR approved for
        §1926.___(a) and Appendix A of §1926.___.
        (a)   55, 55
        (b)   58, 59
        (c)   61, 65
        (d)   66, 68
        Answer: (a) 55, 55. See §1926.6(g)

Subpart A §1926.6(h)
16.   The following material is available for purchase from the **American National Standards
        Institute (ANSI)**, 25 West 43rd Street, ___ Floor, New York, NY 10036;telephone 212-
        642-4900, ,fax:212-302-1286; e-mail: *info@ansi.org*. Web site: *http://www.ansi.org/*.
        (a)   Second
        (b)   Third
        (c)   Fourth
        (d)   Fifth
        Answer: (c) Fourth. See §1926.6(h)

Subpart A §1926.6(h)(1)
17.   The following material is available for purchase from the American National Standards
        Institute (**ANSI**), 25 West 43rd Street, Fourth Floor, New York, NY 10036;telephone
        212-642-4900, ,fax:212-302-1286; e-mail: *info@ansi.org*. Web site:
        http://www.ansi.org/.
        ANSI A10.3-1970, Safety Requirements for Explosive-Actuated Fastening Tools, IBR
        approved for § 1926.302(__).
        (a)   d
        (b)   e
        (c)   f
        (d)   i
        Answer: (b) e. See §1926.6(h)(1)

Subpart A §1926.6(h)(2) incorporation by reference

18.   The following material is available for purchase from the American National Standards Institute (ANSI), 25 West 43rd Street, Fourth Floor, New York, NY 10036;telephone 212-642-4900, ,fax:212-302-1286; e-mail: *info@ansi.org*. Web site: *http://www.ansi.org/*.
ANSI A10.4-1963, Safety Requirements for Workmen's Hoists, IBR approved for § 1926.552(__).
(a)   a
(b)   b
(c)   c
(d)   d
Answer: (c) c. See §1926.6(h)(2)

Subpart A §1926.6(h)(3)

19.   The following material is available for purchase from the American National Standards Institute (ANSI), 25 West 43rd Street, Fourth Floor, New York, NY 10036;telephone 212-642-4900, ,fax:212-302-1286; e-mail: *info@ansi.org*. Web site: *http://www.ansi.org/*.
ANSI A10.4-1969, Safety Requirements for Material Hoists, IBR approved for § 1926.552(__).
(a)   a
(b)   b
(c)   c
(d)   d
Answer: (b) b. See §1926.6(h)(3)

Subpart A §1926.6(h)(4)

20.   The following material is available for purchase from the American National Standards Institute (ANSI), 25 West 43rd Street, Fourth Floor, New York, NY 10036;telephone 212-642-4900, ,fax:212-302-1286; e-mail: *info@ansi.org*. Web site: *http://www.ansi.org/*.
ANSI A11.1-1965 (R1970), Practice for Industrial Lighting, IBR approved for § 1926.56(__).
(a)   a
(b)   b
(c)   c
(d)   d
Answer: (b) b. See §1926.6(h)(4)

Subpart A §1926.6(h)(5) Incorporation by reference

21.   The following material is available for purchase from the American National Standards Institute (ANSI), 25 West 43rd Street, Fourth Floor, New York, NY 10036;telephone 212-642-4900, ,fax:212-302-1286; e-mail: *info@ansi.org*. Web site: *http://www.ansi.org/*.
       ANSI A17.1-1965, Elevators, Dumbwaiters, Escalators, and Moving Walks, IBR approved for § 1926.552(___).
       (a)   a
       (b)   b
       (c)   c
       (d)   d
       Answer: (d) d. See §1926.6(h)(5)

Subpart A §1926.6(h)(6)

22.   The following material is available for purchase from the American National Standards Institute (ANSI), 25 West 43rd Street, Fourth Floor, New York, NY 10036;telephone 212-642-4900, ,fax:212-302-1286; e-mail: *info@ansi.org*. Web site: *http://www.ansi.org/*.
       ANSI A17.1a-1967, Elevators, Dumbwaiters, Escalators, and Moving Walks Supplement, IBR approved for § 1926.552(___).
       (a)   a
       (b)   b
       (c)   c
       (d)   d
       Answer: (d) d. See §1926.6(h)(6)

Subpart A §1926.6(h)(7)

23.   The following material is available for purchase from the American National Standards Institute (ANSI), 25 West 43rd Street, Fourth Floor, New York, NY 10036;telephone 212-642-4900, ,fax:212-302-1286; e-mail: *info@ansi.org*. Web site: *http://www.ansi.org/*.
       ANSI A17.1b-1968, Elevators, Dumbwaiters, Escalators, and Moving Walks Supplement, IBR approved for § 1926.552(___).
       (a)   a
       (b)   b
       (c)   c
       (d)   d
       Answer: (d) d. See §1926.6(h)(7)

Subpart A §1926.6(h)(8) Incorporation by reference

24.   The following material is available for purchase from the American National Standards Institute (ANSI), 25 West 43rd Street, Fourth Floor, New York, NY 10036;telephone 212-642-4900, ,fax:212-302-1286; e-mail: *info@ansi.org*. Web site: *http://www.ansi.org/*.
ANSI A17.1c-1969, Elevators, Dumbwaiters, Escalators, and Moving Walks Supplement, IBR approved for § 1926.552(___).
(a)   a
(b)   b
(c)   c
(d)   d
Answer: (d) d. See §1926.6(h)(8)

Subpart A §1926.6(h)(9)

25.   The following material is available for purchase from the American National Standards Institute (ANSI), 25 West 43rd Street, Fourth Floor, New York, NY 10036;telephone 212-642-4900, ,fax:212-302-1286; e-mail: *info@ansi.org*. Web site: *http://www.ansi.org/*.
ANSI A17.1c-1970, Elevators, Dumbwaiters, Escalators, and Moving Walks Supplement, IBR approved for § 1926.552(___).
(a)   a
(b)   b
(c)   c
(d)   d
Answer: (d) d. See §1926.6(h)(9)

DU VALLS
OSHA 1926 Subpart A—General
Instructors Manual Master Study Guide Series
Test Set 1926.6 ANSI Incorporation by reference

Subpart A §1926.6(h)(10) Incorporation by reference
1. The following material is available for purchase from the American National Standards Institute (ANSI), 25 West 43rd Street, Fourth Floor, New York, NY 10036;telephone 212-642-4900, ,fax:212-302-1286; e-mail: *info@ansi.org*. Web site: *http://www.ansi.org/*.
   ANSI A17.2-1960, Practice for the Inspection of Elevators (**Inspectors Manual**), IBR approved for § 1926.552(__).
   (a)   a
   (b)   b
   (c)   c
   (d)   d
   Answer: (d) d. See §1926.6(h)(10)

Subpart A §1926.6(h)(11)
2. The following material is available for purchase from the American National Standards Institute (ANSI), 25 West 43rd Street, Fourth Floor, New York, NY 10036;telephone 212-642-4900, ,fax:212-302-1286; e-mail: *info@ansi.org*. Web site: *http://www.ansi.org/*.
   ANSI A17.2a-1965, Practice for the Inspection of Elevators (**Inspectors Manual**) Supplement, IBR approved for § 1926.552(__).
   (a)   a
   (b)   b
   (c)   c
   (d)   d
   Answer: (d) d. See §1926.6(h)(11)

Subpart A §1926.6(h)(12)
3. The following material is available for purchase from the American National Standards Institute (ANSI), 25 West 43rd Street, Fourth Floor, New York, NY 10036;telephone 212-642-4900, ,fax:212-302-1286; e-mail: *info@ansi.org*. Web site: *http://www.ansi.org/*.
   ANSI A17.2b-1967, Practice for the Inspection of Elevators (**Inspectors Manual**) Supplement, IBR approved for § 1926.552(__).
   (a)   a
   (b)   b
   (c)   c
   (d)   d
   Answer: (d) d. See §1926.6(h)(12)

Subpart A §1926.6(h)(13) Incorporation by reference

4.   The following material is available for purchase from the American National Standards Institute (ANSI), 25 West 43rd Street, Fourth Floor, New York, NY 10036;telephone 212-642-4900, ,fax:212-302-1286; e-mail: *info@ansi.org*. Web site: *http://www.ansi.org/*.
   ANSI A92.2-1969, Vehicle Mounted Elevating and Rotating Work Platforms**, IBR** approved for §§ 1926.553(__) and 1926.553(__).
   (a)   a, b
   (b)   b, c
   (c)   c, d
   (d)   d, e
   Answer: (a) a, b. See §1926.6(h)(13)

Subpart A §1926.6(h)(14)

5.   The following material is available for purchase from the American National Standards Institute (ANSI), 25 West 43rd Street, Fourth Floor, New York, NY 10036;telephone 212-642-4900, ,fax:212-302-1286; e-mail: *info@ansi.org*. Web site: *http://www.ansi.org/*.
   ANSI B7.1-1970, Safety Code for the Use, Care, and Protection of Abrasive Wheels, IBR approved for §§ 1926.57(__), 1926.303(__), 1926.303(__), 1926.303(__), and 1926.303(__).
   (a)   a, b, c, d
   (b)   b, c, d, g
   (c)   c, d , e, f
   (d)   g, b, c, d
   Answer: (d) g, b, c, d. See §1926.6(h)(14)

Subpart A §1926.6(h)(15)

6.   The following material is available for purchase from the American National Standards Institute (ANSI), 25 West 43rd Street, Fourth Floor, New York, NY 10036;telephone 212-642-4900, ,fax:212-302-1286; e-mail: *info@ansi.org*. Web site: *http://www.ansi.org/*.
   ANSI B7.1-1957, Safety Code for Conveyors, Cableways, and related Equipment. IBR approved for § 1926.555(__).
   (a)   a
   (b)   b
   (c)   c
   (d)   d
   Answer: (a) a. See §1926.6(h)(15)

Subpart A §1926.6(h)(16) Incorporation by reference
7.   The following material is available for purchase from the American National Standards Institute (ANSI), 25 West 43rd Street, Fourth Floor, New York, NY 10036;telephone 212-642-4900, ,fax:212-302-1286; e-mail: *info@ansi.org*. Web site: *http://www.ansi.org/*.
ANSI B7.1-1957, Safety Code for Powered Industrial Trucks, IBR approved for § 1926.602(__).
(a)   a
(b)   b
(c)   c
(d)   d
Answer: (c) c. See §1926.6(h)(16)

Subpart A §1926.6(h)(17)
8.   The following material is available for purchase from the American National Standards Institute (ANSI), 25 West 43rd Street, Fourth Floor, New York, NY 10036;telephone 212-642-4900, ,fax:212-302-1286; e-mail: *info@ansi.org*. Web site: *http://www.ansi.org/*.
ANSI 36.1-1950 (R1971), Rubber Insulating Line Hose, IBR approved for § 1926.951(__).
(a)   a
(b)   b
(c)   c
(d)   d
Answer: (a) a. See §1926.6(h)(17)

Subpart A §1926.6(h)(18)
9.   The following material is available for purchase from the American National Standards Institute (ANSI), 25 West 43rd Street, Fourth Floor, New York, NY 10036;telephone 212-642-4900, ,fax:212-302-1286; e-mail: *info@ansi.org*. Web site: *http://www.ansi.org/*.
ANSI 36.2-1950 (R1971), Rubber Insulating Hoods, IBR approved for § 1926.951(__).
(a)   a
(b)   b
(c)   c
(d)   d
Answer: (a) a. See §1926.6(h)(18)

Subpart A §1926.6(h)(19)
10.   The following material is available for purchase from the American National Standards Institute (ANSI), 25 West 43rd Street, Fourth Floor, New York, NY 10036;telephone 212-642-4900, ,fax:212-302-1286; e-mail: *info@ansi.org*. Web site: *http://www.ansi.org/*.
ANSI 36.4-1971, Rubber Insulating Blankets, IBR approved for § 1926.951(__).
(a)   a
(b)   b
(c)   c
(d)   d
Answer: (a) a. See §1926.6(h)(19)

Subpart A §1926.6(h)(20) Incorporation by reference

11.   The following material is available for purchase from the American National Standards Institute (ANSI), 25 West 43rd Street, Fourth Floor, New York, NY 10036;telephone 212-642-4900, ,fax:212-302-1286; e-mail: *info@ansi.org*. Web site: *http://www.ansi.org/*.
ANSI 36.5-1971, Rubber Insulating Sleeves, IBR approved for § 1926.951(__).

(a)   a
(b)   b
(c)   c
(d)   d
Answer: (a) a. See §1926.6(h)(20)

Subpart A §1926.6(h)(21)

12.   The following material is available for purchase from the American National Standards Institute (ANSI), 25 West 43rd Street, Fourth Floor, New York, NY 10036;telephone 212-642-4900, ,fax:212-302-1286; e-mail: *info@ansi.org*. Web site: *http://www.ansi.org/*.
ANSI 36.6-1971, Rubber Insulating Gloves, IBR approved for § 1926.951(__).

(a)   a
(b)   b
(c)   c
(d)   d
Answer: (a) a. See §1926.6(h)(21)

Subpart A §1926.6(h)(22)

13.   The following material is available for purchase from the American National Standards Institute (ANSI), 25 West 43rd Street, Fourth Floor, New York, NY 10036;telephone 212-642-4900, ,fax:212-302-1286; e-mail: *info@ansi.org*. Web site: *http://www.ansi.org/*.
ANSI 36.6-1971, Rubber Insulating Matting for Use Around Electrical Apparatus, IBR approved for § 1926.951(__).

(a)   a
(b)   b
(c)   c
(d)   d
Answer: (a) a. See §1926.6(h)(22)

Subpart A §1926.6(h)(23)

14.   The following material is available for purchase from the American National Standards Institute (ANSI), 25 West 43rd Street, Fourth Floor, New York, NY 10036;telephone 212-642-4900, ,fax:212-302-1286; e-mail: *info@ansi.org*. Web site: *http://www.ansi.org/*.
ANSI O1.1-1961, Safety Code for Woodworking machinery, IBR approved for § 1926.304(__).

(a)   d
(b)   e
(c)   f
(d)   g
Answer: (c) f. See §1926.6(h)(23)

Subpart A §1926.6(h)(24) Incorporation by reference

15.   The following material is available for purchase from the American National Standards Institute (ANSI), 25 West 43rd Street, Fourth Floor, New York, NY 10036;telephone 212-642-4900, ,fax:212-302-1286; e-mail: *info@ansi.org*. Web site: *http://www.ansi.org/*.
        ANSI Z35.1-1968, Specifications for Accident Prevention Signs; IBR approved for sec. 1926.___(b), (c), and 1(i).
        (a)   200
        (b)   201
        (c)   202
        (d)   203
        Answer: (a) 200. See §1926.6(h)(24)

Subpart A §1926.6(h)(24)

16.   The following material is available for purchase from the American National Standards Institute (ANSI), 25 West 43rd Street, Fourth Floor, New York, NY 10036;telephone 212-642-4900, ,fax:212-302-1286; e-mail: *info@ansi.org*. Web site: *http://www.ansi.org/*.
        ANSI Z35.1-1968, Specifications for Accident Prevention Signs; IBR approved for sec. 1926.___(b), (c), and 1(i). Copies available for ___ from the IHS Standards Store, 15 Inverness Way East, Englewood, CO 80112; telephone: 1-877-413-5184; Web site: *www.global.ihs.com*.
        (a)   200, purchase
        (b)   201, reading
        (c)   202, study
        (d)   203, examination
        Answer: (a) 200, purchase. See §1926.6(h)(24)

Subpart A §1926.6(h)(25)

17.   The following material is available for purchase from the American National Standards Institute (ANSI), 25 West 43rd Street, Fourth Floor, New York, NY 10036;telephone 212-642-4900, ,fax:212-302-1286; e-mail: *info@ansi.org*. Web site: *http://www.ansi.org/*.
        ANSI Z35.2-1968, Specifications for Accident Prevention Tags, IBR approved for §1926.___(i).
        (a)   200
        (b)   201
        (c)   202
        (d)   203
        Answer: (a) 200. See §1926.6(h)(25)

Subpart A §1926.6(h)(26) Incorporation by reference

18. The following material is available for purchase from the American National Standards Institute (ANSI), 25 West 43rd Street, Fourth Floor, New York, NY 10036;telephone 212-642-4900, ,fax:212-302-1286; e-mail: *info@ansi.org*. Web site: *http://www.ansi.org/*.
    ANSI Z49.1-1967, Safety in Welding and Cutting, IBR approved for §1926.350( ).
    (a)   i
    (b)   j
    (c)   k
    (d)   l
    Answer: (a) i. See §1926.6(h)(26)

Subpart A §1926.6(h)(27)

19. **ANSI Z53.1-1967** (also referred to as ANSI ___), Safety Code for Marking Physical Hazards, IBR approved for Sec. 1926.200(c). Copies available for purchase from IHS Standards Store, 15 Inverness Way east, Englewood, CO 80112; telephone: 1-877-413-5184; Web site: *www.global.ihs.com*.
    (a)   Z53.1-1950
    (b)   Z53.1-1965
    (c)   Z53.1-1967
    (d)   Z53.2-1967
    Answer: (c) Z53.1-1967. See §1926.6(h)(27)

Subpart A §1926.6(h)(28)

20. **ANSI 2535.1-2006 (R2011),** Safety Colors ___ July 19, 2011; IBR approved for §1926.200(c).
    (a)   restored
    (b)   reaffirmed
    (c)   replaced
    (d)   registered
    Answer: (b) reaffirmed. See §1926.6(h)(28)

Subpart A §1926.6(h)(28)(i)

21. **ANSI 2535.1-2006 (R2011),** Safety Colors reaffirmed July 19, 2011; IBR approved for §1926.200(c). Copies available for purchase from the
    American National Standards Institute's ___ Store, 25 West 43rd Street, 4th Floor, New York, NY 10036;telephone 212-642-4980; Web site: *http://www.webstore.ansi.org/*;
    (a)   National
    (b)   Web
    (c)   e- Standards
    (d)   International
    Answer: (c) e-Standards. See §1926.6(h)(28)(i)

Subpart A §1926.6(h)(28)(ii) Incorporation by reference

22. **ANSI 2535.1-2006 (R2011),** Safety Colors reaffirmed July 19, 2011; IBR approved for §1926.200(c). Copies available for purchase from the IHS Standards Store, ___Inverness Way east, Englewood, CO 80112;telephone: 877-413-5184; Web site: *http://www.global.ihs.com/* or
    - (a) 12
    - (b) 13
    - (c) 14
    - (d) 15

    Answer: (d) 15. See §1926.6(h)(28)(ii)

Subpart A §1926.6(h)(28)(iii)

23. **ANSI 2535.1-2006 (R2011),** Safety Colors reaffirmed July 19, 2011; IBR approved for §1926.200(c). Copies available for purchase from the IHS Standards Store, 15 Inverness Way east, Englewood, CO 80112;telephone: 877-413-5184; Web site: *http://www.global.ihs.com/* or TechStreet Store, 3916 ___, Ann Arbor, MI 40108; telephone: 877-699-9277; Web site: *www.techstreet.com*.
    - (a) Dearborn Drive
    - (b) River Rouge Road
    - (c) Ranchero Dr.
    - (d) Lakeshore Dr.

    Answer: (c) Ranchero Dr. See §1926.6(h)(28)(iii)

Subpart A §1926.6(h)(29)

24. **ANSI 2535.2-2006 (R2011),** Environmental and Facility Safety Signs, ___ September 15, 2011, IBR approved for §1926.200(b), (c), and (i). Copies available from the:
    - (a) issued
    - (b) published
    - (c) approved
    - (d) certified.

    Answer: (b) published. See §1926.6(h)(29)

Subpart A §1926.6(h)(29)(i)

25. **ANSI 2535.2-2006 (R2011),** Environmental and Facility Safety Signs, published September 15, 2011, IBR approved for §1926.200(b), (c), and (i). Copies available from the: American National Standards Institute's ___ Store, 25 West 43rd Street, 4th Floor, New York, NY 10036;telephone 212-642-4980; Web site: *http://www.webstore.ansi.org/*;
    - (a) e-Standards
    - (b) ACI
    - (c) ASTM
    - (d) On Line

    Answer: (a) e-Standards. See §1926.6(h)(29)(i)

Subpart A §1926.6(h)(29)(ii) Incorporation by reference

26. **ANSI 2535.2-2006 (R2011),** Environmental and Facility Safety Signs, published September 15, 2011, IBR approved for §1926.200(b), (c), and (i). Copies available from the: IHS Standards Store, ___ Inverness Way East, Englewood, CO 80112;telephone: 877-413-5184; Web site: *http://www.global.ihs.com/* or

    (a)   14
    (b)   15
    (c)   16
    (d)   17

Answer: (b) 15. See §1926.6(h)(29)(ii)

Subpart A §1926.6(h)(29)(iii)

27. **ANSI 2535.2-2006 (R2011),** Environmental and Facility Safety Signs, published September 15, 2011, IBR approved for §1926.200(b), (c), and (i). Copies available from IHS Standards Store, 15 Inverness Way East, Englewood, CO 80112;telephone: 877-413-5184; Web site: *http://www.global.ihs.com/* or
TechStreet Store, 3916 ___, Ann Arbor, MI 40108; telephone: 877-699-9277; Web site: *www.techstreet.com*.

    (a)   Dearborn Drive
    (b)   River Rouge Road
    (c)   Ranchero Dr.
    (d)   Lakeshore Dr.

Answer: (c) Ranchero Dr. See §1926.6(h)(29)(iii)

Subpart A §1926.6(h)(30)

28. **ANSI 2535.5-2011,** Safety Tags and Barricade Tapes (for Temporary Hazards), published September 15, 2011, including ___, November 14, 2011; IBR approved for §1926.200(h) and (i). Copies available for purchase from the:

    (a)   Excreta
    (b)   E-Notes
    (c)   Special notes
    (d)   Errata

Answer: (d) Errata. See §1926.6(h)(30)

Subpart A §1926.6(h)(30)(i)

29. **ANSI 2535.5-2011,** Safety Tags and Barricade Tapes (for Temporary Hazards), published September 15, 2011, including Errata, November 14, 2011; IBR approved for §1926.200(h) and (i). Copies available for purchase from the: American National Standards Institute's ___ Store, 25 West 43rd Street, 4th Floor, New York, NY 10036;telephone 212-642-4980; Web site: *http://www.webstore.ansi.org/*;

    (a)   e-Standards
    (b)   ACI
    (c)   ASTM
    (d)   On Line

Answer: (a) e-Standards. See §1926.6(h)(30)(i)

Subpart A §1926.6(h)(30)(ii) Incorporation by reference
30. **ANSI 2535.5-2011,** Safety Tags and Barricade Tapes (for Temporary Hazards), published September 15, 2011, including Errata, November 14, 2011; IBR approved for §1926.200(h) and (i). Copies available for purchase from the: IHS Standards Store, 15 Inverness Way ___, Englewood, CO 80112; telephone: 877-413-5184; Web site: *http://www.global.ihs.com/* or
    (a) North
    (b) East
    (c) South
    (d) West
    Answer: (b) East. See §1926.6(h)(30)(ii)

Subpart A §1926.6(h)(30)(ii)
31. **ANSI 2535.5-2011,** Safety Tags and Barricade Tapes (for Temporary Hazards), published September 15, 2011, including Errata, November 14, 2011; IBR approved for §1926.200(h) and (i). Copies available for purchase from the: IHS Standards Store, 15 Inverness Way East, Englewood, CO 80112; telephone: 877-413-5184; Web site: *http://www.global.ihs.com/* or
    (a) North
    (b) East
    (c) South
    (d) West
    Answer: (b) East. See §1926.6(h)(30)(ii)

Subpart A §1926.6(h)(30)(iii)
32. **ANSI 2535.2-2006 (R2011),** Environmental and Facility Safety Signs, published September 15, 2011, IBR approved for §1926.200(b), (c), and (i). Copies available from IHS Standards Store, 15 Inverness Way East, Englewood, CO 80112;telephone: 877-413-5184; Web site: *http://www.global.ihs.com/* or TechStreet Store, 3916 ___, Ann Arbor, MI 40108; telephone: 877-699-9277; Web site: *www.techstreet.com*.
    (a) Dearborn Drive
    (b) River Rouge Road
    (c) Ranchero Dr.
    (d) Lakeshore Dr.
    Answer: (c) Ranchero Dr. See §1926.6(h)(30)(iii)

Subpart A §1926.6(h)(31)
33. **ANSI Z87.1-1968,** Practice for Occupational Education Eye and Face protection, IBR approved for §1926.___.
    (a) 102(a)
    (b) 103(b)
    (c) 104(c)
    (d) 105(d)
    Answer: (a) 102(a). See §1926.6(h)(31)

Subpart A §1926.6(h)(32) Incorporation by reference

34.   American National Standards Institute (ANSI) Z89.1-2009, American National Standard for Industrial Head Protection, approved ___, 2009; IRB approved for Sec. 1926.100(b)(1)(i).
   (a)   January 1, 2009
   (b)   January 15, 2009
   (c)   January 26, 2009
   (d)   February 1, 2009
   Answer: (c) January 16, 2009. See §1926.6(h)(32)

Subpart A §1926.6(h)(32)

35.   American National Standards Institute (ANSI) Z89.1-2009, American National Standard for Industrial Head Protection, approved January 26, 2009; IRB approved for Sec. 1926.100(b)(1)(i). Copies of ANSI Z89.1-2009 are available for purchase only from the ___, 1901 North Moore Street, Arlington, VA 22209-1762; telephone : 703-525-1695; fax: 703-528-2348; Web site: *www.safetyequipment.org*.
   (a)   International Safety Equipment Association
   (b)   United States Industrial Testing Association (USITA)
   (c)   Institute of National Workman Safety (INWS)
   (d)   National Industrial Safety Institute (NISI)
   Answer: (a) International Safety Equipment Association. See §1926.6(h)(32)

Subpart A §1926.6(h)(33)

36.   American National Standards Institute (ANSI) Z89.1-2009, American National Standard for Industrial Head Protection, approved January 26, 2009, 2009; IRB approved for Sec. 1926.100(b)(1)(ii). Copies of ANSI Z89.1-2009 are available for purchase only from the ___, 1901 North Moore Street, Arlington, VA 22209-1762; telephone : 703-525-1695; fax: 703-528-2348; Web site: *www.safetyequipment.org*.
   (a)   1926.100(b)(1)(i)
   (b)   1926.100(b)(1)(ii)
   (c)   1926.100(b)(1)(iii)
   (d)   1926.100(b)(1)(iv)
   Answer: (b) 1926.100(b)(1)(ii). See §1926.6(h)(33)

Subpart A §1926.6(h)(34)

37.   American National Standards Institute (ANSI) Z89.1-2009, American National Standard for Industrial Head Protection, approved January 26, 2009, 2009; IRB approved for Sec. 1926.100(b)(1)(ii). Copies of ANSI Z89.1-2009 are available for purchase only from the ___, 1901 North Moore Street, Arlington, VA 22209-1762; telephone : 703-525-1695; fax: 703-528-2348; Web site: *www.safetyequipment.org*.
   (a)   1926.100(b)(1)(i)
   (b)   1926.100(b)(1)(ii)
   (c)   1926.100(b)(1)(iii)
   (d)   1926.100(b)(1)(iv)
   Answer: (c) 1926.100(b)(1)(iii). See §1926.6(h)(34)

Subpart A §1926.6(h)(35) Incorporation by reference
38.   Subpart A §1926.6(h)(35) is ___.
    (a)   [Revoked]
    (b)   [Rescinded]
    (c)   [Removed]
    (d)   [Reserved]
    Answer: (d) [Reserved]. See §1926.6(h)(35)

A Ficus Tree Publishing LLC. Quick Notes Page

DU VALLS
OSHA 1926 Subpart A—General
Instructors Manual Master Study Guide Series
Test Set 1926.6 A3 ASTM Incorporation by reference

Subpart A §1926.6(j) Incorporation by reference

1. The following material is available for purchase from the American Society for Testing and Materials (ASTM), ASTM International , ___ Barr Harbor Drive PO Box C700, West Conshohocken, PA, 19428-2959; telephone: 610-832-9585; fax: 610-832-9555; e-mail: *service@astm.org*.
    (a)   100
    (b)   150
    (c)   200
    (d)   250
    Answer: (a) 100. See §1926.6(j)

Subpart A §1926.6(j)(1)

2. ASTM A370-1968, Methods and Definitions for mechanical Testing and Steel products, IBR approved for §1926.___(f).
    (a)   1000
    (b)   1001
    (c)   1002
    (d)   1003
    Answer: (b) 1001. See §1926.6(j)(1)

Subpart A §1926.6(j)(2)

3. ASTM B117-1964 ___ Hour Test, IBR approved for §1926.959(a).
    (a)   10
    (b)   25
    (c)   50
    (d)   100
    Answer: (c) 50. See §1926.6(j)(2)

Subpart A §1926.6(j)(3)

4. ASTM ___, Standard Method of Test for Flash Point by the Tag Closer Tester, IBR approved for §1926.155(i).
    (a)   D56-1969
    (b)   D57-1969
    (c)   D58-1969
    (d)   D59-1969
    Answer: (a) D56-1969. See §1926.6(j)(3)

Subpart A §1926.6(j)(4) ASTM Incorporation by reference

5.   ASTM ___, Standard Method of Test for Flash Point by the Pensky Marthens Closed Tester, IBR approved for §1926.155(i).
    (a)   D91-1969
    (b)   D92-1969
    (c)   D93-1969
    (d)   D94-1969
    Answer: (a) D93-1969. See §1926.6(j)(4)

Subpart A §1926.6(k) ASABE

6.   The following material is available for purchase from the American Society of Agriculture and Biological Engineers (ASABE), 2950 ___ Road, St. Joseph, MI 49085; telephone: 269-429-0300; fax: 269-429-3852; e-mail: hq@sabe.org. Web site: *http://www.asabe.org/*:
    (a)   Reid
    (b)   Davis
    (c)   Brunel
    (d)   Rockwell
    Answer: (a) Reid. See §1926.6(j)(5)

Subpart A §1926.6(k) ASABE

7.   The following material is available for purchase from the American Society of Agriculture and Biological Engineers (ASABE), 2950 ___ Road, St. Joseph, MI 49085; telephone: 269-429-0300; fax: 269-429-3852; e-mail: hq@sabe.org. Web site: *http://www.asabe.org/*:
    (a)   Reid
    (b)   Niles
    (c)   Miles
    (d)   Rockwell
    Answer: (b) Niles. See §1926.6(k)

Subpart A §1926.6(k)(1) ASAE

8.   ASAE R313.1-1971, Soil Cone Penetrometer, reaffirmed ___, IBR approved for §1926.1002(e).
    (a)   1975
    (b)   1985
    (c)   1995
    (d)   2005
    Answer: (a) 1975. See §1926.6(k)(1)

DU VALLS
OSHA 1926 Subpart A—General
Instructors Manual Master Study Guide Series
Test Set 1926.6 ASME Incorporation by reference

Subpart A §1926.6(l)

1.	The following material is available for purchase from the American Society of Mechanical Engineers (ASME), ___ Park Avenue, New York, NY 10016; Telephone:1-800-843-2763; fax:973-882-1717; e-mail: *infocentral@asme.org*. Web site *http://www.asme.org/*:
	(a)	One
	(b)	Two
	(c)	Three
	(d)	Five
	Answer: (c) Three. See §1926.6(l)

Subpart A §1926.6(l)(1) Incorporation by reference

2.	ASME 830.2-2005, Overhead and Gantry Cranes (Top Running Bridge, single or Multiple Girder, Top Running Trolley Hoist), issued ___ ("ASME 830.2-2005"), IBR approved for §1926.1438(b).
	(a)	December 13, 2005
	(b)	December 30, 2005
	(c)	January 1, 2006
	(d)	January 5, 2006
	Answer: (b) December 30, 2005. See §1926.6(l)(1)

Subpart A §1926.6(l)(2)

3.	ASME 830.2-2004, Mobile and Locomotive Cranes, issued ___ ("ASME 830.5-2004"), IBR approved for §§1926.1414(b); 1926.1414(e); 1926.1433(b).
	(a)	September 27, 2004
	(b)	October 1, 2004
	(c)	December 13, 2004
	(d)	January 5, 2005
	Answer: (a) September 27, 2004. See §1926.6(l)(2)

Subpart A §1926.6(l)(3)

4.	ASME 830.7-2001, Base-Mounted Drum Hoists, issued ___ ("ASME 830.7-2001"), IBR approved for §1926.1436(e).
	(a)	September 27, 2001
	(b)	October 1, 2001
	(c)	December 13, 2001
	(d)	January 21, 2002
	Answer: (d) January 21, 2002. See §1926.6(l)(2)

Subpart A §1926.6(l) ASME Incorporation by reference

5.   ASME 830.14-2004, Side Boom Tractors, issued Sept. 20, 2004 ("ASME 830.14-2004"), IBR approved for §1926.___.

      (a)   1440(a)
      (b)   1440(b)
      (c)   1440(c)
      (d)   1440(d)
      Answer: (c) 1440(c). See §1926.6(l)

Subpart A §1926.6(l)

6.   ASME Boiler and Pressure Vessel Code, Section ___, 1968, IBR approved for §§1926.152(i), 1926.306(a), and 1926.603(a).

      (a)   V
      (b)   VI
      (c)   VII
      (d)   VIII
      Answer: (d) VIII. See §1926.6(l)

Subpart A §1926.6(l) 6

7.   ASME Power Boilers. Section ___, 1968, IBR approved for §1926.603(a).

      (a)   I
      (b)   II
      (c)   III
      (d)   IV
      Answer: (a) I. See §1926.6(l) 6

DU VALLS
OSHA 1926 Subpart A—General
Instructors Manual Master Study Guide Series
Test Set 1926.6 AWS Incorporation by reference

Subpart A §1926.6(m)

1.   The following material is available for purchase from the American Welding Society (AWS) ___Road, Miami, Florida 33126; telephone: 1-800-443-9353; Web site: *http://www.aws.org/*:
(a)   Puller
(b)   Vandergrift
(c)   LeJeune
(d)   Halsey
Answer: (c) LeJeune. See §1926.6(m)

Subpart A §1926.6(m)

2.   The following material is available for purchase from the American Welding Society (AWS) ___Road, Miami, Florida 33126; telephone: 1-800-443-9353; Web site: *http://www.aws.org/*:
(a)   Puller
(b)   Vandergrift
(c)   LeJeune
(d)   Halsey
Answer: (c) LeJeune. See §1926.6(m)

Subpart A §1926.6(m) 1

3.   AWS D1.1/M:2002, Structural Welding Code—Steel, 18th ed., ANSI approved ___("AWS D1.1/D1.1M:2002), IBR approved for §1926.1436(c).
(a)   July 1, 2001
(b)   Aug. 31, 2001
(c)   Sept. 15, 2001
(d)   Oct. 1, 2001
Answer: (b) Aug. 31, 2001. See §1926.6(m) 1

Subpart A §1926.6(m) 2

4.   ANSI/AWS D14.3-94, Specification for Welding Earthmoving and Construction Equipment, ANSI approved ___ ("ANSI/AWS D14.3-94"), IBR approved for §1926.1436(c).
(a)   Jun. 11, 1993
(b)   June 11, 1993
(c)   Oct. 15, 1993
(d)   Nov. 11, 1993
Answer: (a) Jun. 11, 1993. See §1926.6(m) 2

B. Alphabetical listing.

Subpart A §1926.6(n) incorporation by reference

5. The following material is available for purchase from the **British Standards Institution** (BSI), ___, London, W4 4AL, United Kingdom; telephone: +44 20 8996 9001; fax: +44 20 8996 7001; e-mail *cservices@bsigroup.com*, Web site: *http://www.bsigroup.com/*:
    (a)   389 Chestershire Road
    (b)   389 Chiswick High Road
    (c)   389 Old Bailey Road
    (d)   389 Trafalgar Square Place
    Answer: (b) 389 Chiswick High Road. See §1926.6(n)

Subpart A §1926.6(n) 1

6. **BS** EN 13000: 2004, Cranes-Mobile Cranes, published ___ ("BS EN 13000:2004) IBR approved for §1926.1433(c).
    (a)   Jan. 4, 2006
    (b)   Aug. 31, 2006
    (c)   Sept. 15, 2006
    (d)   Oct. 1, 2006
    Answer: (a) Jan 4, 2006. See §1926.6(n) 1

Subpart A §1926.6(n) 2

7. BS EN 14439:2006, Cranes-Safety-Tower Cranes, published ___ ("BS EN 14439:2006") IBR approved for §1926.1433(c).
    (a)   Jan. 4, 2006
    (b)   Aug. 31, 2006
    (c)   Sept. 15, 2006
    (d)   Oct. 1, 2006
    Answer: (a) Jan 4, 2006. See §1926.6(n) 2

Subpart A §1926.6(o)

8. The following material is available for purchase from the **Bureau of Reclamation**, United States Department of the Interior, ___Street, NW., Washington DC 20240; telephone 202-208-4501; Web site: *http://www.usbr.gov/*:
    (a)   1849 A
    (b)   1849 B
    (c)   1849 C
    (d)   1849 D
    Answer: (c) 1849 C. See §1926.6(o)

Subpart A §1926.6(o) 1 Incorporation by reference. Bureau of Reclamation

9. The following material is available for purchase from the Bureau of Reclamation, United States Department of the Interior, ___Street, NW., Washington DC 20240; telephone 202-208-4501; Web site: *http://www.usbr.gov/*: Safety and Health Regulations for Construction, Part ___, Sept. 1971, IBR approved for §1926.1433(c).
    (a)   I
    (b)   II
    (c)   III
    (d)   V
    Answer: (b) II. §1926.6(o) 1

C. Alphabetical listing. California
Subpart A §1926.6(p)

10.   The following material is available for purchase from the California Department of
       industrial Relations, ___ Golden Gate Avenue, San Francisco CA 94102; telephone:
       (415) 703-5070; e-mail: *info@dir.ca.gov*; Web site *http://www.dir.ca.gov/*:
       (a)   445
       (b)   446
       (c)   447
       (d)   448
       Answer: (a) 445. See §1926.6(p)

Subpart A §1926.6(p) 1

11.   The following material is available for purchase from the California Department of
       industrial Relations, ___ Golden Gate Avenue, San Francisco CA 94102; telephone:
       (415) 703-5070; e-mail: *info@dir.ca.gov*; Web site *http://www.dir.ca.gov/*:
       1926.6 p 1. Construction Safety Orders, IRB approved §1926.___(f)
       (a)   445, 1000
       (b)   446, 1001
       (c)   447, 1002
       (d)   448, 1003
       Answer: (a) 445, 1000. See §1926.6(p) 1

Subpart A §1926.6(p) 1

12.   Subparts 1926.6 q, r, s, and t are listed as ___.
       (a)   [Removed]
       (b)   [Moved]
       (c)   [Reserved]
       (d)   [Inactive]
       Answer: (c) [Reserved]. See §1926.6 q, r, s, t.

A Ficus Tree Publishing LLC. Quick Notes Page

DU VALLS
OSHA 1926 Subpart A—General
Instructors Manual Master Study Guide Series
Test Set 1926.6 Federal Highway Administration
Incorporation by reference

F. Alphabetical listing. Federal

Subpart A §1926.6(u) Incorporation by reference. Federal Highway Administration

1. The following material is available for purchase from the Federal Highway
    Administration, united states Department of Transportation, ___New Jersey Ave., SE.,
    Washington, DC 20590; telephone: 202-366-4000; Web site: *http://www.fhwa.dot.gov/*:
    (a)   1200
    (b)   1300
    (c)   1400
    (d)   1500
    Answer: (a) 1200. See §1926.6(u)

Subpart A §1926.6 (u) 1

2. The following material is available for purchase from the Federal Highway
    Administration, united states Department of Transportation, 1200 New Jersey Ave., SE.,
    Washington, DC 20590; telephone: 202-366-4000; Web site: *http://www.fhwa.dot.gov/*:
    Manual on Uniform Traffic Control Devices (MUTCO) Part ___, Standards and Guides
    for Traffic Controls for Street and Highway Construction, Maintenance, Utility, and
    Incident Management Operation, 1988 Edition, Revision 3, September 3, 1993; IRB
    approved for sec. Sec. 1926.200(g), and 1926.202.
    (a)   VI
    (b)   VII
    (c)   VIII
    (d)   IX
    Answer: (a) VI. See §1926.6 u 1

Subpart A §1926.6 (u) 1

3. The following material is available for purchase from the Federal Highway
    Administration, united states Department of Transportation, 1200 New Jersey Ave., SE.,
    Washington, DC 20590; telephone: 202-366-4000; Web site:
    http://www.osha.gov/doc/hightway_workzones/mutcd/index.html.
    Manual on Uniform Traffic Control Devices (MUTCO) Part ___, Standards and Guides
    for Traffic Controls for Street and Highway Construction, Maintenance, Utility, and
    Incident Management Operation, 1988 Edition, Revision 3, September 3, 1993; IRB
    approved for sec. Sec. 1926.200(g), and 1926.202. Electronic copies of MUTCD, 1988
    Edition, Revision ___ are available for downloading at
    http://mutcd.fhwa.dot.gov/kno-milliennium_12.18.00.htm.
    (a)   VI
    (b)   VII
    (c)   VIII
    (d)   IX
    Answer: (a) VI. See §1926.6 u 1

Subpart A §1926.6 (u) 2 Federal Highway Administration

4.   The following material is available for purchase from the Federal Highway Administration, United States Department of Transportation, 1200 New Jersey Ave., SE., Washington, DC 20590; telephone: 202-366-4000; Web site: *http://www.osha.gov/doc/hightway_workzones/mutcd/index.html*.

Manual on Uniform Traffic Control Devices (MUTCD), Dec. 2000, IBR approved for sec. Sec. 1926.201(a), and 1926.202. Electronic copies of MUTCD ___ are available for downloading at *http://mutcd.fhwa.dot.gov/kno-milliennium_12.18.00.htm*.

(a)   1995
(b)   2000
(c)   2001
(d)   2004
Answer: (b) 2000. See §1926.6 u 2

G. Alphabetical listing.

     Subpart A §1926.6 Incorporation by reference. General Services Administration

Subpart A §1926.6 (v)

5.   The following material is available for purchase from the General Services Administration (GSA), ___ F Street, NW., Washington, DC 20405; telephone: 202-501-0800; Web site: *http://www.gsa.gov/*:

(a)   1776
(b)   1785
(c)   1800
(d)   2001
Answer: (c) 1800. See §1926.6 v

Subpart A §1926.6 (v) 1

6.   The following material is available for purchase from the General Services Administration (GSA), ___ F Street, NW., Washington, DC 20405; telephone: 202-501-0800; Web site: *http://www.gsa.gov/*:

QQ-P-416, Federal Specification Plating Cadmium (electrodeposited), IBR approved for §1926.___(e)

(a)   1776, 102
(b)   1785, 103
(c)   1800, 104
(d)   2001, 105
Answer: (c) 1800, 104. See §1926.6 v 1

I. Alphabetical listing. §1926.6 IME Incorporation by reference

Subpart A §1926.6 (w)
7.   The following material is available for purchase from the Institute of Makers of
        Explosives (IME), ___, 19th Street, NW., Suite310, Washington, DC 20036; telephone:
        202-249-9280; fax: 202-429-9280; e-mail: *info@ime.org*. Web site: *http://www.ime.org/*:
        (a)   1100
        (b)   1110
        (c)   1111
        (d)   1120
        Answer: (d) 1120. See §1926.6 w

Subpart A §1926.6 (w) 1
8.   The following material is available for purchase from the Institute of Makers of
        Explosives (IME), ___, 19th Street, NW., Suite310, Washington, DC 20036; telephone:
        202-249-9280; fax: 202-429-9280; e-mail: *info@ime.org*. Web site: *http://www.ime.org/*:
        IME Pub. No 2, American Table of Distances for Storage of Explosives, ___, IBR
        approved for §1926.914(a)
        (a)   1100, Jun.1, 1964
        (b)   1110, Jun. 3, 1964
        (c)   1111, Jun. 4, 1964
        (d)   1120, Jun. 5, 1964
        Answer: (d) 1120, Jun. 5, 1964. See §1926.6 w 1

Subpart A §1926.6 (w) 2
9.   The following material is available for purchase from the Institute of Makers of
        Explosives (IME), ___, 19th Street, NW., Suite310, Washington, DC 20036; telephone:
        202-249-9280; fax: 202-429-9280; e-mail: *info@ime.org*. Web site: *http://www.ime.org/*:
        IME Pub. No 20, Radio Frequency Range--A Potential Hazard in the Use of Electric
        Blasting Caps, IBR approved for §1926.900(k)
        (a)   1100, Jan. 12, 1968
        (b)   1110, Feb. 1968
        (c)   1111, Feb. 14, 1968
        (d)   1120, Mar. 1968
        Answer: (d) 1120, Mar. 1968. See §1926.6 w 2

ISO Incorporation by reference

Subpart A §1926. 6
10.   The following material is available for purchase from the International Organization for
        Standardization (ISO), ___, ch. de la Voie Creuse, Case postale 56, CH-1211 Geneva 20,
        Switzerland; telephone: +41 22 749 01 11; fax: +41 22 733 34 30; Web site
        http://www.iso.org/:
        (a)   1
        (b)   2
        (c)   3
        (d)   4
        Answer: (a) 1. See §1926.6

Subpart A §1926.6 (x)1

11. The following material is available for purchase from the International Organization for Standardization (**ISO**), 1, ch. de la Voie Creuse, Case postale 56, CH-1211 Geneva 20, Switzerland; telephone: +41 22 749 01 11; fax: +41 22 733 34 30; Web site http://www.iso.org/:
    ISO 11660-1:2008(E), Cranes--Access, guards and restraints--Part ___ : General, 2d ed., Feb. 15, 2008 ("ISO 11660-1:2008(E)"), IBR approved for §1926.1423(c)/
    (a)   1
    (b)   2
    (c)   3
    (d)   4
    Answer: (a) 1. See §1926.6 1

Subpart A §1926.6 (x) 2

12. The following material is available for purchase from the International Organization for Standardization (ISO), 1, ch. de la Voie Creuse, Case postale 56, CH-1211 Geneva 20, Switzerland; telephone: +41 22 749 01 11; fax: +41 22 733 34 30; Web site http://www.iso.org/:
    ISO 11660-2:1994(E), Cranes--Access, guards and restraints--Part ___ : Mobile cranes, 1994 ("ISO 11660-2:1994(E)"), IBR approved for §1926.1423(c)/
    (a)   1
    (b)   2
    (c)   3
    (d)   4
    Answer: (b) 2. See §1926.6 2

Subpart A §1926.6 (x) 3

13. The following material is available for purchase from the International Organization for Standardization (ISO), 1, ch. de la Voie Creuse, Case postale 56, CH-1211 Geneva 20, Switzerland; telephone: +41 22 749 01 11; fax: +41 22 733 34 30; Web site http://www.iso.org/:
    ISO 11660-3:1994(E), Cranes--Access, guards and restraints--Part ___: Tower cranes, 2d ed., Feb. 15, 2008("ISO 11660-2:1994(E)"), IBR approved for §1926.1423(c)/
    (a)   1
    (b)   2
    (c)   3
    (d)   4
    Answer: (c) 3. See §1926.6 (x) 3

N. Alphabetical listing. **Subpart A §1926.6 NFPA Incorporation by reference**

Subpart A §1926.6 (y)

14. The following material is available for purchase from the **National Fire Protection Association** (NFPA), 1 Batterymarch Park, ___, MA 02169; telephone: 617-770-3000: Web site: *http://www.nfpa.org/*:
    (a)   Boston
    (b)   Quincy
    (c)   Washington
    (d)   Springfield
    Answer: (b) Quincy. See §1926.6 (y)

A Ficus Tree Publishing LLC., Educational - Technical Publication

Subpart A §1926.6 (y)(1)

15.   The following material is available for purchase from the National Fire Protection
       Association (NFPA), 1 Batterymarch Park, Quincy, MA 02169; telephone: 617-770-
       3000: Web site: *http://www.nfpa.org/*:
       NFPA 10A-1970, Maintenance and Use of Portable Fire Extinguishers, IRB approved
       for §1926.150(c)
       (a)   100(a)
       (b)   125(b)
       (c)   150(c)
       (d)   185(d)
       Answer: (c) 150(c). See §1926.6(y)(1)

Subpart A §1926.6 (y)(2)

16.   The following material is available for purchase from the National Fire Protection
       Association (NFPA), 1 Batterymarch Park, Quincy, MA 02169; telephone: 617-770-
       3000: Web site: *http://www.nfpa.org/*:
       NFPA 13-1969, Standard for the Installation of Sprinkler Systems, IBR approved
       for §1926.___.
       (a)   100(b)
       (b)   125(c)
       (c)   152(d)
       (d)   185(e)
       Answer: (c) 152(d). See §1926.6 (y)(2)

Subpart A §1926.6 (y)(3)

17.   The following material is available for purchase from the National Fire Protection
       Association (NFPA), 1 Batterymarch Park, Quincy, MA 02169; telephone: 617-770-
       3000: Web site: *http://www.nfpa.org/*:
       NFPA ___, The Flammable and Combustible Liquid Code, IBR approved for
       §1926.152(c).
       (a)   30-1968
       (b)   30-1969
       (c)   30-1980
       (d)   30-1983
       Answer: (b) 30-1969. See §1926.6 (y)(3)

Subpart A §1926.6 (y)(4)

18.   The following material is available for purchase from the National Fire Protection
       Association (NFPA), 1 Batterymarch Park, Quincy, MA 02169; telephone: 617-770-
       3000: Web site: *http://www.nfpa.org/*:
       NFPA ___, Standard for Fire Doors and Windows, Class E or F Openings, IBR approved
       for §1926.152(b).
       (a)   80-1967
       (b)   80-1968
       (c)   80-1969
       (d)   80-1970
       Answer: (d) 80-1970. See §1926.6 (y)(4)

N. Alphabetical listing. Subpart A §1926.6 NFPA Incorporation by reference

Subpart A §1926.6 (y)(5)

19.   The following material is available for purchase from the National Fire Protection Association (NFPA), 1 Batterymarch Park, Quincy, MA 02169; telephone: 617-770-3000: Web site: *http://www.nfpa.org/*:
NFPA ___, Standard Methods of Fire Test of Building Construction and Material, IRB approved for §§1926.152(b) and 1926.155(f).
(a)   251-1969
(b)   251-1970
(c)   251-1971
(d)   252-1971
Answer: (a) 251-1969. See §1926.6 (y)(5)

Subpart A §1926.6 (y)(6)

20.   The following material is available for purchase from the National Fire Protection Association (NFPA), 1 Batterymarch Park, Quincy, MA 02169; telephone: 617-770-3000: Web site: *http://www.nfpa.org/*:
NFPA ___, Standard for Tank Vehicles for Flammable and Combustible Liquids, IRB approved for §1926.152(g).
(a)   385-1966
(b)   385-1967
(c)   385-1968
(d)   385-1969
Answer: (a) 385-1966. See §1926.6 (y)(6)

Subpart A §1926.6 (z) is [Reserved]

P. Alphabetical listing. PCSA Incorporation by reference

Subpart A §1926.6 (aa)

21.   The following material is available for purchase from the Power Crane and Shovel Association (PCSA), ___ W. Washington Street, Suite 2400, Milwaukee, WI 53214; telephone: 1-800-369-2310; fax: 414-272-1170; Web site: *http://www.aem.org/CBC/ProdSpec/PCSA/*:
(a)   6734
(b)   6735
(c)   6736
(d)   6737
Answer: (d) 6737. See §1926.6 (aa)

P. Alphabetical listing.
Subpart A §1926.6 (aa)(1)
22.   The following material is available for purchase from the Power Crane and Shovel
       Association (PCSA), 6737 W. Washington Street, Suite 2400, Milwaukee, WI 53214;
       telephone: 1-800-369-2310; fax: 414-272-1170; Web site:
       http://www.aem.org/CBC/ProdSpec/PCSA/:
       PCSA Std. No. 1, Mobile Crane and Excavator Standards, 1968, IRB approved for
       §1926.___(b)
       (a)   601
       (b)   602
       (c)   603
       (d)   604
       Answer: (b) 602 See §1926.6 (aa)(1)

Subpart A §1926.6 (aa)(2)
23.   The following material is available for purchase from the Power Crane and Shovel
       Association (PCSA), 6737 W. Washington Street, Suite 2400, Milwaukee, WI 53214;
       telephone: 1-800-369-2310; fax: 414-272-1170; Web site:
       http://www.aem.org/CBC/ProdSpec/PCSA/:
       PCSA Std. No. 2, Mobile Hydraulic Crane Excavator Standards, 1968 ("PCSA Std. No. 2
       (1968)"), IRB approved for §§1926.602(b), 1926.1433(a), and 1926.___(a).
       (a)   1500
       (b)   1501
       (c)   1503
       (d)   1504
       Answer: (b) 1501 See §1926.6 (aa)(2)

Subpart A §1926.6 (aa)(3)
24.   The following material is available for purchase from the Power Crane and Shovel
       Association (PCSA), 6737 W. Washington Street, Suite 2400, Milwaukee, WI 53214;
       telephone: 1-800-369-2310; fax: 414-272-1170; Web site:
       http://www.aem.org/CBC/ProdSpec/PCSA/:
       PCSA Std. No. 3, Mobile Hydraulic Excavator Standards, 1969, IRB approved for
       §1926.___(b).
       (a)   600
       (b)   601
       (c)   602
       (d)   603
       Answer: (c) 602 See §1926.6 (aa)(3)

Subpart A §1926.6 (bb)[Reserved]

Subpart A §1926.6 (cc)[Reserved]

S. Alphabetical listing. SAE Incorporation by reference.

Subpart A §1926.6 (dd)

25.   The following material is available for purchase from the Society of Automotive Engineers (SAE), 400 Commonwealth Drive, ___, PA15096; telephone: 1-877-606-7323; fax: 724-776-0790; Web site: *http://www.sae.org/*:
  (a)   Pittsburgh
  (b)   Harrisburg
  (c)   Warrendale
  (d)   Revere
  Answer: (c) Warrendale. See §1926.6 (dd)

Subpart A §1926.6 (dd)(1)

26.   The following material is available for purchase from the Society of Automotive Engineers (SAE), 400 Commonwealth Drive, Warrendale, PA15096; telephone: 1-877-606-7323; fax: 724-776-0790; Web site: *http://www.sae.org/*:
  SAE 1970 Handbook, IBR approved for §1926.___(b)
  (a)   600
  (b)   601
  (c)   602
  (d)   603
  Answer: (c) 602. See §1926.6 (dd)(1)

Subpart A §1926.6 (dd)(2)

27.   The following material is available for purchase from the Society of Automotive Engineers (SAE), 400 Commonwealth Drive, Warrendale, PA15096; telephone: 1-877-606-7323; fax: 724-776-0790; Web site: *http://www.sae.org/*:
  SAE 1971 Handbook, IBR approved for §1926.___(b)
  (a)   1000
  (b)   1001
  (c)   1002
  (d)   1003
  Answer: (b) 1001. See §1926.6 (dd)(2)

Subpart A §1926.6 (dd)(3)

28.   The following material is available for purchase from the Society of Automotive Engineers (SAE), 400 Commonwealth Drive, Warrendale, PA15096; telephone: 1-877-606-7323; fax: 724-776-0790; Web site: *http://www.sae.org/*:
  SAE ___-1971, Trucks and Wagons, Handbook, IBR approved for §1926.601(a)
  (a)   J163
  (b)   J164
  (c)   J165
  (d)   J166
  Answer: (d) 3166. See §1926.6 (dd)(3)

A Ficus Tree Publishing LLC., Educational - Technical Publication

SAE Incorporation by reference

Subpart A §1926.6 (dd)(4)

29. The following material is available for purchase from the Society of Automotive Engineers (SAE), 400 Commonwealth Drive, Warrendale, PA15096; telephone: 1-877-606-7323; fax: 724-776-0790; Web site: *http://www.sae.org/*:

    SAE ___-1970, Protective Enclosures--Test Procedures and Performance Requirements, IBR approved for §1926.1002(a).
    (a)   J166
    (b)   J167
    (c)   J168
    (d)   J169
    Answer: (d) J168. See §1926.6 (dd)(4)

Subpart A §1926.6 (dd)(5)

30. The following material is available for purchase from the Society of Automotive Engineers (SAE), 400 Commonwealth Drive, Warrendale, PA15096; telephone: 1-877-606-7323; fax: 724-776-0790; Web site: *http://www.sae.org/*:

    SAE J185(reaf. May 2003), Access Systems for Off-Road Machines, reaffirmed May 2003 ("SAE J185 (May ___")), Protective Enclosures--Test Procedures and Performance Requirements, IBR approved for §1926.1423(c).
    (a)   1993
    (b)   1994
    (c)   1995
    (d)   1997
    Answer: (a) 1993. See §1926.6 (dd)(5)

Subpart A §1926.6 (dd)(6)

31. The following material is available for purchase from the Society of Automotive Engineers (SAE), 400 Commonwealth Drive, Warrendale, PA15096; telephone: 1-877-606-7323; fax: 724-776-0790; Web site: *http://www.sae.org/*:

    SAE J236, Self-Propelled Graders, IBR approved for §1926.___(a).
    (a)   601
    (b)   602
    (c)   603
    (d)   604
    Answer: (b) 602. See §1926.6 (dd)(6)

Subpart A §1926.6 (dd)(7)

32. The following material is available for purchase from the Society of Automotive Engineers (SAE), 400 Commonwealth Drive, Warrendale, PA15096; telephone: 1-877-606-7323; fax: 724-776-0790; Web site: *http://www.sae.org/*:

    SAE ___, Front End Loaders and Dozers, IBR approved for §1926.602(a).
    (a)   J237
    (b)   J238
    (c)   J239
    (d)   J240
    Answer: (a) J237. See §1926.6 (dd)(7)

A Ficus Tree Publishing LLC., Educational - Technical Publication

Subpart A §1926.6 (dd)(8)
33. The following material is available for purchase from the Society of Automotive Engineers (SAE), 400 Commonwealth Drive, Warrendale, PA15096; telephone: 1-877-606-7323; fax: 724-776-0790; Web site: *http://www.sae.org/*:
SAE ___(b)-1971, Self-Propelled Scrapers, IBR approved for §1926.602(a).
(a) J317
(b) J318
(c) J319
(d) J320
Answer: (b) 602. See §1926.6 (dd)(8)

Subpart A §1926.6 (dd)(9)
34. The following material is available for purchase from the Society of Automotive Engineers (SAE), 400 Commonwealth Drive, Warrendale, PA15096; telephone: 1-877-606-7323; fax: 724-776-0790; Web site: *http://www.sae.org/*:
SAE ___(a)-1971, Minimum Performance Criteria for Roll-Over Protective Structure for Rubber-Tired, Self-Propelled Scrapers, IBR approved for §1926.1001(h).
(a) J320
(b) J321
(c) J322
(d) J323
Answer: (a) J320. See §1926.6 (dd)(9)

Subpart A §1926.6 (dd)(10)
35. The following material is available for purchase from the Society of Automotive Engineers (SAE), 400 Commonwealth Drive, Warrendale, PA15096; telephone: 1-877-606-7323; fax: 724-776-0790; Web site: *http://www.sae.org/*:
SAE ___(a)-1970, Fenders for Pneumatic-Tired Earthmoving Haulage Equipment, IBR approved for §1926.602(a).
(a) J320
(b) J321
(c) J322
(d) J323
Answer: (b) J321. See §1926.6 (dd)(10)

Subpart A §1926.6 (dd)(11)
36. The following material is available for purchase from the Society of Automotive Engineers (SAE), 400 Commonwealth Drive, Warrendale, PA15096; telephone: 1-877-606-7323; fax: 724-776-0790; Web site: *http://www.sae.org/*:
SAE ___(a)-1970, Operator Protection for Agricultural and Light Industrial Tractors, IBR approved for §1926.602(a).
(a) J330
(b) J331
(c) J332
(d) J333
Answer: (b) J333. See §1926.6 (dd)(11)

Subpart A §1926.6 (dd)(11)

37.	The following material is available for purchase from the Society of Automotive Engineers (SAE), 400 Commonwealth Drive, Warrendale, PA15096; telephone: 1-877-606-7323; fax: 724-776-0790; Web site: *http://www.sae.org/*:
SAE ___(a)-1970, Seat Belts for Construction Equipment, IBR approved for §1926.602(a).
(a)	J385
(b)	J386
(c)	J387
(d)	J388
Answer: (b) J386. See §1926.6 (dd)(11)

Subpart A §1926.6 (dd)(12)

38.	The following material is available for purchase from the Society of Automotive Engineers (SAE), 400 Commonwealth Drive, Warrendale, PA15096; telephone: 1-877-606-7323; fax: 724-776-0790; Web site: *http://www.sae.org/*:
SAE ___-1971, Minimum Performance Criteria for Roll-Over Protective Structure for Rubber-Tired Front End Loaders and Rubber-Tired Dozers, IBR approved for §1926.1001(h).
(a)	J392
(b)	J393
(c)	J394
(d)	J395
Answer: (b) J394. See §1926.6 (dd)(12)

Subpart A §1926.6 (dd)(13)

39.	The following material is available for purchase from the Society of Automotive Engineers (SAE), 400 Commonwealth Drive, Warrendale, PA15096; telephone: 1-877-606-7323; fax: 724-776-0790; Web site: *http://www.sae.org/*:
SAE ___-1971, Minimum Performance Criteria for Crawler Tractors and Loaders, IBR approved for §1926.1001(h).
(a)	J392
(b)	J393
(c)	J394
(d)	J395
Answer: (b) J395. See §1926.6 (dd)(14)

Subpart A §1926.6 (dd)(14)

40.	The following material is available for purchase from the Society of Automotive Engineers (SAE), 400 Commonwealth Drive, Warrendale, PA15096; telephone: 1-877-606-7323; fax: 724-776-0790; Web site: *http://www.sae.org/*:
SAE ___-1971, Minimum Performance Criteria for Motor Graders, IBR approved for §1926.1001(h).
(a)	J394
(b)	J395
(c)	J396
(d)	J397
Answer: (d) J397. See §1926.6 (dd)(15)

Subpart A §1926.6 (dd)(15)

41.   The following material is available for purchase from the Society of Automotive Engineers (SAE), 400 Commonwealth Drive, Warrendale, PA15096; telephone: 1-877-606-7323; fax: 724-776-0790; Web site: *http://www.sae.org/*:
SAE ___-1969, Critical Zone Characteristics and Dimensions for Operators of Construction and Industrial Machinery, IBR approved for §1926.1001(h).
(a)   J394
(b)   J395
(c)   J396
(d)   J397
Answer: (d) J397. See §1926.6 (dd)(15)

Subpart A §1926.6 (dd)(16)

42.   The following material is available for purchase from the Society of Automotive Engineers (SAE), 400 Commonwealth Drive, Warrendale, PA15096; telephone: 1-877-606-7323; fax: 724-776-0790; Web site: *http://www.sae.org/*:
SAE ___a-1964, Tractor Mounted Side Boom, 1964 ("SAE___a-1964"), IBR approved for §1926.1501(a).
(a)   J743, J743
(b)   J744, J744
(c)   J745, J745
(d)   J756, J746
Answer: (a) J743, J743. See §1926.6 (dd)(16)

Subpart A §1926.6 (dd)(17)

43.   The following material is available for purchase from the Society of Automotive Engineers (SAE), 400 Commonwealth Drive, Warrendale, PA15096; telephone: 1-877-606-7323; fax: 724-776-0790; Web site: *http://www.sae.org/*:
SAE ___-1966, Lifting Crane Wire-Rope Strength Factors, 1966 ("SAE ___ -1966"), IBR approved for §1926.1501(a).
(a)   J957, J957
(b)   J958, J958
(c)   J959, J959
(d)   J960, J960
Answer: (c) J959, J959. See §1926.6 (dd)(17)

Subpart A §1926.6 (dd)(18)

44.   The following material is available for purchase from the Society of Automotive Engineers (SAE), 400 Commonwealth Drive, Warrendale, PA15096; telephone: 1-877-606-7323; fax: 724-776-0790; Web site: *http://www.sae.org/*:
SAE ___ (rev. Jun. 2003), Lattice Boom Cranes-Method of Test, revised Jun. 2003 ("SAE ___ (Jun. 2003)"), IBR approved for §1926.1433(c).
(a)   J957, J987
(b)   J958, J988
(c)   J959, J989
(d)   J960, J990
Answer: (c) J987, J987. See §1926.6 (dd)(18)

Subpart A §1926.6 (dd)(19)
45.   The following material is available for purchase from the Society of Automotive Engineers (SAE), 400 Commonwealth Drive, Warrendale, PA15096; telephone: 1-877-606-7323; fax: 724-776-0790; Web site: *http://www.sae.org/*:
SAE ___ (rev. Nov. 1993), Cantilevered Boom Crane Structures-Method of Test, revised Nov. 1993 ("SAE ___ (Nov. 1993)"), IBR approved for §1926.1433(c).
(a)   J1001, J1001
(b)   J1063, J1063
(c)   J1075, J1075
(d)   J2005, J2005
Answer: (b) J1063, J1063. See §1926.6 (dd)(19)

Subpart A §1926.6 Incorporation by reference
U.S. Army Corps of Engineers

Subpart A §1926.6 (cc)
46.   The following material is available for purchase from the United States Army Corps of Engineers, ___ G Street, NW, Washington, DC 20314; telephone: 202-761-0011; e-mail: *hq-publicaffairs@usace.army.mil/*; Web site: *http://www.usace.army.mil/*:
(a)   440
(b)   441
(c)   442
(d)   443
Answer: (b) 441. See §1926.6 (cc)

Subpart A §1926.6 (cc) 1
47.   The following material is available for purchase from the United States Army Corps of Engineers, 441 G Street, NW, Washington, DC 20314; telephone: 202-761-0011; e-mail: *hq-publicaffairs@usace.army.mil/*; Web site: *http://www.usace.army.mil/*:
EM-___-1-1, General Safety Requirements, Mar. 1967, IBR approved for §1926.1000(f).
(a)   214
(b)   357
(c)   385
(d)   387
Answer: (c) 385. See §1926.6 (cc) 1

§1926.6 Incorporation by reference - Standards Resellers

Subpart A §1926.6 (ff)
48.   The following material is available for purchase from standards resellers such as the Document Center Inc., ___ Industrial Road, Suite 9, Belmont , CA 94002; telephone: 650-591-7600; fax: 650-591-7617; e-mail: *info@document-center.com/*;
Web site: *http://www.document-center.com/*.
(a)   111
(b)   222
(c)   333
(d)   555
Answer: (a) 111. See §1926.6 (ff)

§1926.6 Incorporation by reference - Standards Resellers

Subpart A §1926.6 (ff) 1

49.   The following material is available for purchase from standards resellers such as the Document Center Inc., 111 Industrial Road, Suite 9, Belmont , CA 94002; telephone: 650-591-7600; fax: 650-591-7617; e-mail: *info@document-center.com/*; Web site: *http://www.document-center.com/*.
ANSI B15.1-1953 (R1958), Safety Code for mechanical Power-Transmission Apparatus, revised 1958, IBR approved for §§ 1926.300(b)(2) and 1926.___(a).
(a)   125
(b)   150
(c)   175
(d)   201
Answer: (b) 150. See §1926.6 (ff) 1

Subpart A §1926.6 (ff) 2

50.   The following material is available for purchase from standards resellers such as the Document Center Inc., 111 Industrial Road, Suite 9, Belmont , CA 94002; telephone: 650-591-7600; fax: 650-591-7617; e-mail: *info@document-center.com/*; Web site: *http://www.document-center.com/*.
ANSI B30.2.0-1967, Safety Code for Overhead and Gantry cranes, approved May 4, 1967, IBR approved for § 1926.___(d).
(a)   1252
(b)   1501
(c)   1753
(d)   2012
Answer: (b) 1501. See §1926.6 (ff) 2

Subpart A §1926.6 (ff) 3

51.   The following material is available for purchase from standards resellers such as the Document Center Inc., 111 Industrial Road, Suite 9, Belmont , CA 94002; telephone: 650-591-7600; fax: 650-591-7617; e-mail: *info@document-center.com/*; Web site: *http://www.document-center.com/*.
ANSI B30.5-1968, Crawler, locomotive, and truck Cranes, approved ___, IBR approved for §§ 1926.1433(a), 1926.1501(a) and 1926.1501(b).___(d).
(a)   Dec. 11, 1954
(b)   Dec. 13, 1955
(c)   Dec. 16, 1968
(d)   Dec. 24, 1973
Answer: (c) Dec. 16, 1968. See §1926.6 (ff) 3

§1926.6 Incorporation by reference - Standards Resellers

Subpart A §1926.6 (ff)

52.   The following material is available for purchase from standards resellers such as the Document Center Inc., 111 Industrial Road, Suite 9, Belmont , CA 94002; telephone: 650-591-7600; fax: 650-591-7617; e-mail: *info@document-center.com/*;
Web site: *http://www.document-center.com/*.
ANSI B30.6-1969, Safety Code for derricks, approved, ___, IBR approved for
§ 1926.1501(e).

(a)   Dec. 11, 1954
(b)   Dec. 13, 1955
(c)   Dec. 18, 1967
(d)   Dec. 24, 1973
Answer: (c) Dec. 18, 1967. See §1926.6 (ff)

[75 FR 481.31, August 9, 2010; 77 FR 37600, June 22, 2012; 78 FR 35566-35567, June 13, 2013; **78 FR 66641-66642, November 6, 2013**]

A Ficus Tree Publishing LLC. Quick Notes Page

Ficus Tree Publishing LLC. Instructors Manuals

Amazon   Create Space   Kindle

IRS Publications

IRS Publication 15 Employers Tax Guide
Instructors Manual 2014 Edition (IRS Tax Rules and Regulations)

DUVALLS Circular E Employers Tax Guide, Instructors Manual, Master Study Guide Series, 2014 Edition, written for the current IRS Edition, is now available from Amazon.com, in soft cover print-on-demand (P.O.D.) format. This copyrighted work is also available from Kindle and the e-book version from Amazon's Create Space.

This is a comprehensive Instructors Manual with multiple-choice questions set forth generally, in direct sequence to the official U.S. government publication. The multiple-choice questions with answers provide a simplified easy to read, easy to study platform for your students.

The Instructors Manual is designed as the textbook material supplement the specific course required to be upgraded. With very little effort each Instructor now has at their fingertips comprehensive class syllabus material for each new scholastic quarter or semester.

The 2014 Edition provides new information (What's New?), IRS Publication 15, introduced for use in 2014. It is understood that the free IRS Publication 15, Employer's Tax Guide and 2014 tax tables must be used as the primary textbook for this Work.

Important changes to Circular E set forth in the Instructors Manual include the following: What's New? — Same Sex marriage information. the use of gender neutral "Spouse" to replace "Husband and Wife Business" with "Business Owned and Operated By Spouses". Additional information for obtaining Tax Help is provide in the new and expanded "How To Get Tax Help".

Every page from IRS Publication 15, Employers Tax Guide is developed into test type multiple-choice questions with answers. This book contains over 500 pages with over 1500 multiple-choice questions with answers for you, the Instructor, to easily develop your class material.

Ficus Tree Publishing LLC. Instructors Manuals

Amazon   Create Space   Kindle

OSHA Publications for 2014
Instructors Manual 2014 Edition of OSHA
1903
1904
1910
1926

The above listed DUVALLS OSHA Instructors Manuals, 2014 Edition are now available from Amazon.com, in soft cover print-on-demand (P.O.D.) format. The copyrighted works are also available from Kindle and the e-book version from Amazon's Create Space. Professors, Teachers, and Instructors will be notified as our additional Master Study Guide Series become available via the above listed sources.

The Works, our publications, are comprehensive Instructors Manuals with multiple-choice questions set forth generally, in direct sequence to the official Department of Labor, U.S. government publication. The multiple-choice questions with answers provide a simplified easy to read, easy to study platform for your students and for you, the instructor to develop your course material.

The Instructors Manuals are designed as the textbook material for each specific course required for your lecture series. With very little effort you, the Instructor, have at your fingertips the necessary comprehensive class syllabus material for each new scholastic quarter or semester without the accompanying, unnecessary, workload stress.

The work is presented in a generally sequential format that faithfully parallels the official United States Publications. Further, there are no intentional "trick" questions. There are difficult questions for your students to solve but all questions are provided with answers. It is a simple process for your students to follow. Read the sentence, paragraph or passage as written in the text then read and solve the test question. The initial lecture, the reading of the text and the solving of the problem reinforces the basic learning processes.

It is a simple, easy and efficient procedure.

29 CFR OSHA

Part 1903
Inspections, Citations and Proposed Penalties

OSHA Part 1903 provides information to the rules and requirements for Inspections, Citations and Proposed Penalties. This Instructors Manual for 2014 contains approximately 145 pages of information, text, and multiple-choice test type questions. Over 300 questions with answers.

Information provided in the form of multiple-choice test type questions with answers is progressive, generally sequential to the official Part 1903 publication. Information presented relates to the following" Williams-Steiger Act. the General Duty Clause. The conduct of inspections. General enforcement policy. Posting of a notice. Dimensions of posters. Reproductions of posters. Availability of the Act. Authority for inspection. Objection to inspection. Entry not a waiver. Advance notice of inspections. Conduct of inspections.

This work is a Instructors Manual created specifically for OSHA 1903. The intent is to reduce a level of pressure caused by searching documents and records for suitable lecture material.

Part 1904
Recording and Reporting Illnesses and Injuries

OSHA Part 1904 is an important publication for all businesses. As an employer you are responsible. the Instructors Manual contains 208 pages with over 500 questions, soft cover, printed in black and white. Generally sequential test type, multiple-choice questions provided with answers, parallel the official OSHA publication. The multiple-choice questions includes but not limited to the following standards: §1904.1 Subpart A—Purpose. §1904.1Subpart B—Scope. §1904.2 Partial exemption for employers with 10 or fewer employees. §1904.2 Partial exemption for certain industries. §1904.3 Keeping records for more than one agency. §1904 Subpart B App A— Partially Exempt Industries SIC codes. The Decision Tree. §1904.4 Subpart C—Recording criteria. §1904.5 Determination of work-relatedness. §1904.6 Determination of new cases. §1904.7 Subpart C—General recording criteria. §1904.8 —Needlestick and sharps injuries. §1904.9 Recording criteria for cases involving medical removal under OSHA standards. §1904.10—Recording criteria involving hearing loss. §1904.11—Recording criteria for work-related tuberculosis cases. §1904.29 Forms. §1904.30 Multiple business establishments. §1904.31 — Covered employees. §1904.32 Annual summary. §1904.33 Retention and updating, (important - how long must you retain the records)? §1904.34 Change in business ownership. §1904.35 Employee involvement. §1904.36 Prohibition against discrimination. §1904.37 State recordkeeping regulations. §1904.38 Variances from the recordkeeping. §1904.39 reporting fatalities and multiple hospitalization incidents to OSHA. §1904.40 Providing records to government representatives. §1904.41 Annual OSHA injury and illness survey of ten or more employers. §1904.42 Requests from the Bureau of Labor Statistics for data. §1904.43 Summary and posting of 2001 data. §1904.44 Retention and updating of old forms. §1904.45 OMB control numbers under the Paperwork Reduction Act. §1904.46 Definitions.

29 CFR OSHA

Part 1910 Occupational Safety and Health Standards (The Subparts)

Part 1926
Safety and Health Regulations For Construction (The Subparts)

§1926 Subpart A—General

70 pages. A soft cover, fastback binding, printed black and white. Test type multiple-choice questions with answers written in general sequential form to parallel the official Department of Labor publication. Over one hundred questions in this subpart test including test questions for the following: §1926.1 Purpose and scope. §1926.2 Variances from safety and health standards. §1926.3 Inspections - right of entry. §1926.4 Rules of practice for administrative adjudications for enforcement of safety and health standards. §1926.5 OMB control numbers test questions with answers. §1926.6 Incorporation by reference. Both §§ 1926.5 and 1926.6 are frequently overlooked when studying for professional tests. However, questions from this part do appear on professional and licensing examination with greater frequency.

This DUVALLS Master Study Guide Series contains over 70 pages with over 100 multiple-choice questions with answers.

§1926 Subpart B—General Interpretations
(Written, under review and updating)

§ 1926 Subpart C—General Safety and Health Provisions
(Written, under review and updating)

§1926 Subpart D—Occupational Health and Environmental Controls
(Written, under review and updating)

§1926 Subpart E—Personal Protective and Life Saving Equipment
(Written, under review and updating)

§1926 Subpart F—Fire Protection and Prevention
(Written, under review and updating)

§1926 Subpart G—Signs, Signals, and Barricades
(Written, under review and updating)

§1926 Subpart H—Materials Handling, Storage, Use, and Disposal
(Written, under review and updating)

§1926 Subpart I—Tools—Hand and Power
(Written, under review and updating)

January 2014 OSHA 1926 Base Data
Department of Labor

§1926 Subpart J—Welding and Cutting
(Written, under review and updating)

§1926 Subpart K—Electrical
(Written, under review and updating)

§1926 Subpart L—Scaffolds
(Written, under review and updating)

§1926 Subpart M—Fall Protection
(Written, under review and updating)

§1926 Subpart N—Cranes, Derricks, Hoists, Elevators,
Conveyors and Helicopter Operations
(Written, under review and updating)

§1926 Subpart O—Motor Vehicles, Mechanized Equipment, and Marine Operations
(Written, under review and updating)

§1926 Subpart P—Excavations
(Written, under review and updating)

§1926 Subpart Q—Concrete and Masonry Construction
(Written, under review and updating)

§1926 Subpart R—Steel Erection
(Written, under review and updating)

§1926 Subpart S—Underground Constructions, Caissons,
Cofferdams and Compressed Air
(Written, under review and updating)

§1926 Subpart T—Demolition
(Written, under review and updating)

§1926 Subpart U—Blasting and the Use of Explosives
(Unavailable)

§1926 Subpart V—Power Transmission and Distribution
(Written, under review and updating)

January 2014 OSHA 1926 Base Data
Department of Labor

§1926 Subpart W—Rollover Protective Structures,
Overhead Protection
(Written, under review and updating)

§1926 Subpart X—Stairways and Ladders
(Written, under review and updating)

§1926 Subpart Y—Diving
(Written, under review and updating)

§1926 Subpart Z—Toxic and Hazardous Substances
(Written, under review and updating)

§1926 Subpart CC—Cranes and Derricks in Construction
(Written. Under review, updating and editing)

Reminder:

Department of Labor Occupational Safety and Health Administration. 29 CFR Part 1926. [Docket No. OSHA-2007-0066] RIN No. 1218-AC61

Cranes and Derricks in Construction: Underground Construction and Demolition.

Agency: Occupational Safety and Health Administration (OSHA), Labor.

Action: Final rule.

SUMMARY: On August 17, 2012, OSHA issued a notice of proposed rulemaking, as well as a companion direct final rule, that proposed applying the requirements in OSHA's 2010 cranes and derricks construction standard to underground construction work and demolition work. The notice of proposed rulemaking also proposed to correct inadvertent errors in the underground construction and demolition standards. After receiving a comment recommending that OSHA clarify the proposed regulatory text of the demolition standard, OSHA clarified the text and is issuing this final rule to apply the cranes and derricks standard to underground construction work and demolition work.

Date: This final rule is effective May 23, 2013. Petitions for the final rule of this final review are due on June 24, 2013.

www.ingramcontent.com/pod-product-compliance
Lightning Source LLC
LaVergne TN
LVHW081320060426
835509LV00015B/1609